THE SUN HORSE

The Sun Horse

NATIVE VISIONS OF THE NEW WORLD

COLLECTED AND RETOLD BY

Gerald Hausman

LOTUS LIGHT
Twin Lakes, Wisconsin

First Edition

Printed in the United States of America.

Library of Congress Catalog Card Number: 92-71218
Native American/Mythology
        ISBN 0-914955-08-X

LOTUS LIGHT PUBLICATIONS
PO Box 325, Twin Lakes, Wisconsin 53181 USA

CONTENTS

INTRODUCTION

Through Native American Eyes:
The Founding of Turtle Island America

Geologists like to tell us that the basic components of earth, air, water and fire, fused in the crucible of primordial time, formed our world. Native Americans, however, speaking through their religious myths, tell a different tale. Their version of the origin story speaks of a mystical creator, like an energy force, who, in concert with Earth and Sky, created our universe. The result may be the same — out of chaos is born order — but the difference as seen through Indian eyes is not a matter of boiling and cooling and the interchange of light, heat and mass. Rather, it is the bonding of two principles, male and female, mother and father. The Cherokees describe a primary world of water and sky, out of which came Water Beetle, the explorer, who took it upon himself to seek the sacred mud of Mother Earth. The story is told countless ways, but usually, water is made stable by Earth, having union with Father Sky. There is almost always a Great Flood in the mythology of the First People. However, unlike biblical renditions, the native flood is not brought down as a punishment, it is instead a natural outgrowth of "upward pushing" activities. The tendency in Native American origin stories that reveal our earthly beginnings is to show how the earth was made from the shared ideas of the creator, the animate earth and sky, the great water of the sea, man, animal, insect, and all

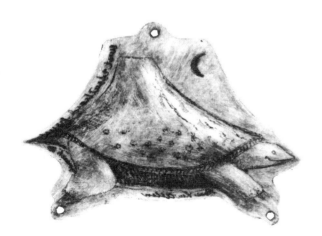

life in between. Four (and sometimes five) worlds dominate the usual tale of rising from lower to upper levels of life. These worlds, or stages of growth, are shown clearly in all Native American myths. As the waters drop, the earth rises, and man and woman emerge as spiritual entities, sharing a balance of power on the spiritual plane of existence.

The visions and dreams recounted in this book point to the way Native Americans have visualized their world for hundreds, even thousands, of years. America, to the Indian, was generally known as Turtle Island. The turtle is the universal symbol of the mother, upon whom the burden of the great shell is carried. The children of the turtle are the children of Mother Nature. They are animal, insect, fish, reptile, amphibian, human. They are are the founders of a world rooted in the belief that all is equal, that oneness is achieved through joining, not separating.

Mythologically, Native Americans have referred to themselves as the children of a creator whose name takes many forms, but whose personal aspect is "a divine and mysterious presence." The elements — earth, air, water, fire — act in unison with the creator, the Great Mystery. The sacred directions — east, west, north and south — are naturally an important part of the paradigm. A Native American man of the past, one who was in touch with the Great Mystery and who knew the four-quarters and the four directions as he knew his own mind would often be called a "mystery man" or in plain terms, a medicine man.

The Sun Horse: Native Visions of the New World begins with the tribes that lived by the great sea, perhaps the earliest explorers of this continent, and concludes, having cycled full circle, with the desert dwellers, who, we are told, came from the mythic North, and settled in the sandy Southwest. The book, then, represents a circle, moving geophysically and mythologically from salt water — the cosmic and microcosmic elemental birthplace — to desert sand, the reposing place of earth-matter, or materiality.

Yet it is the "world beyond," the upper world, that which the Christians call Heaven, which also figures in many Native American myths. The realm of the Sun Horse, a deity of the Navajo, is the sky: "He carries a rainbow in His mouth for a bridle." In the story *The Sun Horse*, the Navajo protagonist sees his earthly quest as one of unifying the dual worlds of earth and sky. And, in each of the stories given here Mother Earth and Father Sky are somehow enjoined.

The world of the visionary from whom these tales come is

not a "mystical world," in the non-Indian sense of that word. For, in Native American myths, as well as the life lived today, Indians do not separate living and doing from thinking. A myth is not merely an amusing tale, but an accurate rendering of spiritual history. If all life is animate to the Indian, then the story is just as alive, the act of storytelling just as real, as the fire that spews from the mouth of the volcano or the rain that blows from the sea. Spiritual life and material wellbeing are together, myth and matter are made one in the telling. Myths are true moments in time and the telling of them makes them come alive again.

The visions that make up this volume are taken from the experiences, past and present, of Native American story-tellers. The voices are the sounds of wind and thunder, mountains and trees and spinning sand. The speakers themselves come from many tribes: Pascagoula, Arawak, Iroquois, Arapaho, Kiowa, Rio Grande Pueblo, Kwakiutl, Cherokee and Navajo. As archivist and writer, I have been gathering Native American stories since 1965. This collection represents the "unshakable stories," those that come back to haunt the listener, time and time again. The title story, *The Sun Horse*, was originally told to me in two parts. The first half was given more than twenty-five years ago. The second half came unexpectedly last spring. When I

asked the storyteller why he had waited so long to relate the whole tale, he informed me that he "had to live through it." In doing so, he gained the experience that is indispensible to the native storyteller who does not tell stories for the purpose of entertainment, but to impart the cardinal truths of the tribe.

excellent storytelling quote.

Gerald Hausman
Tesuque, New Mexico

FOREWORD

In all educational institutions the problem of teaching or interpreting history has fallen to the expertise — or lack thereof — of making history relevant to you and me. The assembly of dates, important names and succession of cultures means only as much as can be applied to life.

As a professor at the Institute of American Indian Arts Museum, I have on occasion taken my students to Bandelier (a National Park Service Prehistoric Indian Center and Museum). Apart from the tourist activities, guided talks and beautiful museum, my students, who are Native American, usually gain a much more lasting impression of this "tiny piece of pre-history" by visiting and just sitting. They listen to the soft breezes through the trees which tell them of stalking deer and the tiny river and hear the laughter of the women who are gathering water. As they feel the pictographs and let their hands sensitively touch the inside of the old ruins, they can hear the drums from the kivas from so long ago.

Gerald Hausman is a unique individual because he, like my students, is quietly sensitive to the world about him. His words are worthy because he can touch the feelings of those he writes about, whether they are of pain, joy, anger, or just life in general.

To be able to record the sense of a site or a skirmish which affected each of us in some way in our history is easily done by description, maps and documentation. To be able to sense the sweat of horses, to feel the fear, pain and exhilaration of the warriors, the residual ghosts and spirits which haunt the area are the unique capabilities of Mr. Hausman. We have listened closely to him. He feels the flying horse manes and the lingering spirits which speak in those winds which touch the trees.

Charles Dailey
Professor of Museum Studies
The Institute of American Indian Arts
Santa Fe

Book One: CHILDREN OF THE SEA

THE BREAD EATERS

The strange music was first heard at the mouth of the Pascagoula River, on a calm, moonless night. Visitors among the Pascagoula Indians would hear the sound of a harp, which would come and go with the wind and tide. A Catholic priest, who had stationed himself among the Indians sometime during the 1700s, claimed that the music was inspired by the Devil. He patiently weaned them, so his journal said, of their heathen ways — The worship of a mermaid who lived in the waters of the Bay. Things went well for the priest until one full moon night, when a woman of the tribe received a vision. After this, the Indians would no longer listen to the priest. He attributed his failure to the ascension of the powers of darkness.

On his deathbed, the priest told his listeners that there was only one way to redeem the lost souls of the Pascagoulas: "At twelve o'clock on Christmas eve, when the moon was at the meridian, a priest must drop a crucifix into the dark waters of the Bay."

This, he said, would save the tribe from further devil-worship and repair their souls unto the Lord. So saying, he died, a broken man.

I, a Pascagoula, have seen many things since the coming of the whites to our land. I have met and talked with the man in black with the long white beard, which our children are so fond of touching.

He wears a loose black dress and carries with him at all times a small silver cross. This, he says, is the source of his magic.

There is magic in the man. Surely it is so, for he speaks our language, and yet no one has taught him one single word. He came among us with knowledge of it. And this impressed our chiefs.

He is solemn, handsome, soft-spoken. When he speaks, we listen. There is much in what he says: He speaks of

the Great Flood. We know of it. Our own priests tell of the time of the rains when the great canoe was prepared and all the animals got into it, except Possum whose tail dragged in the water and lost all of its fur.

The man with the small cross knows this story by heart, and his heart is good in telling it. "The Spirit that moves upon the waters," he says, so sweetly that we can feel the power of his words, and those of his Lord, the Sky-Dweller.

But I am Pascagoula and I do not know how long the man with the pale skin and the silver cross will be upon this earth, any more than I know how long we Bread Eaters will be upon it. Yet he says he knows this, and more. His kind, the whites, he says, will always be here:

They are the chosen children of the Sky-Dweller, he says. Such a thing troubles our people. We pray for a vision. We fast and wait for a sign...

One night I go out into the bay when the moon is full. I ask our Mother who resides in the water what to do. Should we listen to the stranger who has come among us who shares our bread eaten on the rocks it is cooked on?

Suddenly the water dances in the moonlight, the stirring of fish trembles the small dug-out boat, and all at once there is a great commotion of fins. The soft air is full of fish. If I were catching them my arms would not be strong enough to capture even a few, for the fish are all shapes and sizes, and so many they cannot be counted.

The little boat thrashes in the waves, rises and falls, and the fish overleap it. Shark and porpoise, turtle and sea cow, ray and mullet beyond measure. Then the water begins to spin and to go above my head, and the boat goes down into the center of a hole wherein beats the heart of the sea: and there it is calm.

I am alone. The moon is full, I can hear the heart of the sea, beating. Then it is our Mother. I hear singing I have never heard before.

The waves part. It is our Mother. I have heard stories about her, but I have never seen her with my own eyes. She looks grieved as she looks upon me. She stands upon the water with the tail of a fish and the body of a woman. And her hair spreads out into the moonlit water like lovely water-weed.

She does not speak, but a song comes from her lips and I am given to understand it, for her language is the same as ours. She says this: "Come to me, child of the sea. Do not let your people look upon the bell, book or cross of the friendly stranger. For what I am, you are also, and together we are stronger than this man and all of his brothers."

Then she smiled upon me and dropped back into the water of the bay, and her long black, seawater hair spread out upon wet moonlight. Then there was only the watery tangle of her hair, which sank into the foam.

Then even that was gone.

When I told my people what had happened, they listened. But the man with the silver cross grew angry with me, for what I said would not agree with what he said.

"Our Mother would not lie to us," I said to him.

He said, "You will be damned for talking this; you will burn in Hell."

But we know of no such place. Our chiefs say not to listen to him any more, because when he talks, his voice is like a loud wind that rushes upon us, but changes direction often and means nothing. He is not the same after this; I have heard lately that he is sick, that he will die soon.

We live on.

We are Pascagoula, Bread Eaters.

*No one can explain, to this day, why the entire village,
shortly after the death of the priest, walked into the waters
of the Bay, and vanished. Men, women, and children —
the whole tribe. Some say they fled the whites. Some
explain that they retreated from another tribe, perhaps
the Choctaws, who tried to take their land.*

*There are even those who say it was a tribe of Africans,
not Native Americans, who marched into the Bay, fleeing
the tyranny of their white masters. The legend is lost in
the land of its birth, a country of mist, hanging moss,
and madness. There are fisherman who say that if you
go out on a moonlit night into the center of Biloxi Bay,
you will hear the singing. It comes from the water, down
deep. And sometimes, on the full moon of Christmas Eve,
you can feel the water rise and whirl upon the swell, and
there is a sudden froth of fishes, so many you cannot count
them. Then the water subsides, and grows quiet again.*

THE ARAWAK

On the island of Jamaica, where the Arawak people lived, there is a story of a similar sea-goddess. Christopher Columbus, upon his arrival on the island, believed he had truly discovered a paradise on earth. In 1494, he and his men had no trouble conquering the tractable Arawak, who had already been vanquished by the hostile Carib tribe. Time passed and the Spanish overlords grew restless.

What had they come for?

They were not there to collect tariffs from the Indians, but to discover a much nobler treasure: gold.

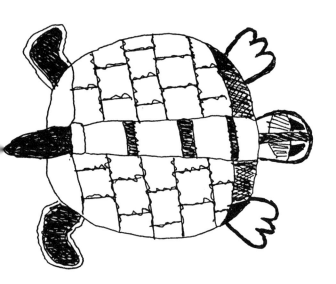

The Arawak let them look and the Spanish peered under every tropical leaf. Meanwhile the Arawak were quiet, they played games and smoked the leaves that grew in their fields. They slept on woven mat beds strung between the trees; they called these *hammocks*, and the Spanish found them very agreeable. The Spanish also enjoyed the smoking-herb, the Indians' barkless dogs and singing children, but they needed to find gold to bring back to Queen Isabella. Otherwise their voyage was worthless.

They became feverish, suffering tropic ills and complaints. But mostly their fever was for the brightness of their golden dream. Somewhere, they knew, it was there. The Arawaks, friendly though they were, had managed to keep this one thing a secret. The gold was there, if they might only crack the mysterious vault of secrecy.

One day a shaman of the Arawak told one of Columbus' men that there was indeed a secret inland river in whose milky water there lived a goddess, half-woman and half-fish. She was lovely to look at, the shaman said, for her hair was longer than her tail.

The men with the hard-pointed hats asked the shaman to take them to the river, so they might see where the fish-woman lived. The shaman took them to the river and what they saw there was far more amazing than they had anticipated.

The fish-woman was there, the very one described by the shaman. She was beautiful to look at, with cream-colored skin and yellow hair. Her lower body was that of a fish, covered with shiny scales, but her hair was filled with the light of the sun and she combed it and caressed it, hour after hour, with a golden comb.

"I must have that comb," the leader of the Columbus party said.

But the shaman shook his head sadly. "That, you cannot have," he said.

The Spaniard became enraged and throwing the shaman aside, dived into the water to catch the fish-woman. Immediately recovering himself, the shaman jumped into the water to stop the mad Spaniard.

Then all three, the fish-woman, the Spaniard, the shaman disappeared under the water.

They were never seen again.

But the story of Spanish greed remains on the island to this day. In the clear-water, where the fresh empties into the salt in the place where the two waters meet, you see her: mermaid, moomah, mother, water-woman, spirit of the water.

> "With a golden comb she combs her hair down so, down so, she seh. Her hair cross her face like a curtain of sun. Now the moomah catch a sailor, if she can, if she can. 'Do you eat fresh or salt?' she say, she seh.
>
> If him say salt, it be alright.
>
> If him say fresh, she kill him. Because where she come from, fresh, fresh. Her comb out her long pretty-pretty hair, Spirit of the Water, Spirit of the Fresh."

In 1548, a Spanish census turned up only 490 Arawaks. By the 17th century, due to slavery and disease, the paradisal people, whose kindness had saved the lives of Columbus and his men, were gone — lost like the Pascagoula in the gold mist of their own legend. Yet the myth of the goddess who looked after them, now told by the ancestors of African slaves on the island, can still be heard, a living reminder of the price of human greed.

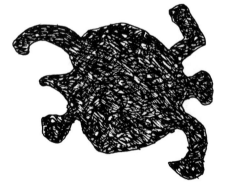

THE RAVEN WATCHER

Along the north Pacific coast of America and Canada, from Vancouver Island to Alaska, Native American tribes carved their myths in cedar. They were known as totem poles and they were of various kinds: some were decorative and heraldic house-poles, others were erected as memorial columns. The interior house-poles were made only by the wealthy; they stood in the center of the lodge, directly behind the fireplace. During the great feasts, known as potlatches, tribesmen felled the trees, rolled them into the water and towed them to their village where, after singing and dancing, the village carver would go to work.

The origin of the totem pole, like the origin of anything, is questionable, but there is a theory that the great poles were not native to the Pacific Northwest. Anthropologists believe they may have come on the tide all the way from Korea. The Native American version of the story is less concerned with where the pole came from than the simple fact that it did, in fact, come.

In the country of the owl, where the moon moves the sea far up into the forest, between the tug of the moon and the tag of the sea, there live the people called Kwakiutl. From the sea they take what is necessary to live: the mud-burrowing clam, the halibut with two eyes on top of its head, the salmon they call Swimmer. And all along the salt-water shores the people are followed by the feathered hunters and scavengers who are hungry for what they have caught. These are the terns and gulls, the cormorants and ravens, the tide-takers and water-watchers.

There is no end to the feasting when Swimmer comes up the tidal river. By hook and by net and by hand the people pull them in. Overhead the cry of the osprey, the cough of the raven, and the loud snore of the feasted bear. The people eat as well off the land as they do the sea. From the land there is bear meat, deer meat, elk meat, and rabbit. From the sea there is cod, halibut, smelt, seal, porpoise, and whale. Seal fat is eaten from a bowl that is carved to look like a seal. In the cold sea the seal oil keeps the blood warm, so the people eat it to keep summer in the blood.

Long, long ago, so the people say, there was a man who had a dream. In this dream, he saw himself stripping bark from the yellow-cedar and giving it to his wife to soak in salt-water, so that, after pounding and separating the bark into strands, it could be woven into cold-weather cloaks.

I am Raven-Watcher. They gave me that name because like Raven, the trickster, I have dreams and things happen. The night I dreamed winter was coming, I saw my woman weaving bark.

The way of the dream led to the sea; I followed it. There was something out in the grey that spoke to me, a tree floating in the water that was not a tree. I saw my name-face, Raven, on the tree. I heard thunder and saw Eagle fly over head, I saw Bear rubbing his back on spruce tree, and far off Cormorant clapping his wing.

I woke and dressed and went down to the shore. The Animal People had spoken, I had listened. Then the long thing on the tide, the tree without bark, clean as a young girl with faces on her skin: Raven, Eagle, Bear, Cormorant, and other faces I did not recognize.

I told the people of the tree.
And everyone agreed it was a good sign.

Salmon   with life and death,
         trusts river
         in spring,
         is born into river
         in the end,
         passes from river into spirit

river realizing
river with purpose
river hosting life
     the circular life of the Salmon
river sang…

one day
bear stops
to talk
with Singing River
wakes her
river with thousand-star eyes
rises to the
furry paws
she sings,
"shhhh, whisper bear, my children, the Salmon they
     are coming"

And everyone agreed it was a good sign.

Thus did the totem pole come to the native people of the Pacific Northwest: the Haida, the Kwakiutl, the Tsimshian, and other tribes who lived near the sea. In the tradition of the house-owner, the totem pole in front of his house bore many legends. House-poles that told stories occasionally depicted the figure of the house-owner himself. Sometimes, so they say, the stories carved in wood showed the face of a person the house-owner wished to ridicule. It all depended on the owner of the pole, the life he led, the places his dreams had taken him.

THE MOTHER AND CHILD

The Seri Indians of Mexico live by the Gulf of the Sea of Cortez in the Baja. It is a dry desert land with water on one side, desert on the other, and a watchful sky burning overhead. At night the coyotes spin their pin-wheel laughter; during the day the sky is patroled by broad-winged hawks and carrion-seeking vultures.

It is a land of no in-between — sharp contrast calls the eye and claims it prisoner. Today, the Seri people live as the rest of the world does, but their art goes back to another time, a time of legend. The Seris carve totems of dark wooden creatures: birds, sharks, animals that live in and around the sea and the desert. The hard, dark wood and the hard dark faces of the carvers are seen around Kino Bay, and you would think — if you were vacationing there by the sea — that these remote, isolate people would know nothing of their distant cousins living in Pueblos in the Southwest. But you would be wrong. A Pueblo veteran from the Vietnam war once told me the following story about his visit to the Seri country.

The world is wide but faith, they say, is wider than the world.

Once I had a family, and land. But first, I had Vietnam. Or, I should say, Vietnam had me. It was after I came back and settled on the land owned by my aunt near the Pueblo that I got a family: a wife and two children.

But it wasn't long before the war and what happened there — perhaps the ghosts of those men I killed in battle — came back to haunt me. I gave up, then, on tribal ways, stopped going to dances. My clan forgot I was living there, my own aunt once passed me on the street, and she did not know me.

But then I didn't know myself. How should anyone else know me? I lost heart, it is that simple. My wife begged me to keep my job at the lumberyard, but it was too far away to walk to work and I couldn't make the car payments and the finance company got the car, and I lost my job. After that, my wife worked and I slept late in the mornings. She would come home in the afternoon with the kids back from play-school, and she'd look everywhere but at me. It was as if I wasn't there.

One time I looked in the mirror and I almost thought I wasn't there because who was there, wasn't me. But some other me had stepped in and taken his place, my place.

After that I didn't care, I got into drugs. Beer and wine, anything that would make me high. The old story. I got to be a bum, a man without a dream, a man without a heart. It happened lightning-fast. One day I was a man, one day I wasn't.

My wife would have taken me back. I just wouldn't go back. What for? For my kids? My kids didn't have a father…. One day I decided to go away, like some old piece of tarpaper that blows off a shack, and the wind carries it away with the dust and the dirt, and it is never seen again.

I bummed my way south, with just the shirt on my back. Lost nights and lonely places, dogs without owners, tumbleweeds, men with eyes dead as cigarette butts, these became the road-map of my soul. One day I woke up in a Dempster-dumpster. My clothes had been cut into fringe, someone had cut my hair off. That was somewhere outside of El Paso. So I said, what the hey… why not go down to old Mexico, just keep hitching until the sky ate up the road, and then the sea ate up the sky, and keep on going.

And keep on going.

Which is what I did.

By the Gulf of the Sea of Cortez, I got so hungry I ate my supper out of a garbage can by the beach. It was there the old man stopped me. He was a dark old man, and he stopped me with a glance. Then he said, "—You, a young man," and shook his head so pitifully that I wanted to cry, because there was something about that old man in his frayed, tweed, cast-off, rich-guy's jacket and his faint white stubble-beard like the frost of a dog's mouth, and his darker-than-mine skin.

The only thing he said to me that day was, "—You, a young man," and he made a thumb-gesture for me to follow him.

I did that, I followed him home.

The old man lived in a beat-up trailer by the sea. A big enough wave could've swallowed the whole thing up in one gulp. There was a clothesline out back and a fire-place of sea-stones in front, and that was pretty much it. He made a simple, honest living carving birds out of black wood. The eyes were hard little seeds he picked off a tree.

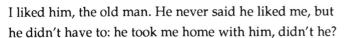
I liked him, the old man. He never said he liked me, but he didn't have to: he took me home with him, didn't he?

For the first few weeks I sat around doing nothing. Watching the old man, mostly. He used to rise at dawn and go into the sea with just his shorts on and wash himself off in the breakers. He never asked me to join him, but one morning, just for the hell of it, I followed him in. The sea was so cold it stung my skin. The old man laughed and laughed.

You'd have thought it was the only funny thing he'd ever seen — me getting wet like that.

Afterwards, I got the chills and rolled around in the hot sand to get warm. For breakfast, he fried some bonito jack. We slept for a little while, then the old man took me on a long hike. We went up a steep cliff that looked out over the Sea of Cortez. The wind really roared up there, and the seagulls screamed.

There was a cave at the very edge of the cliff. You had to lower yourself to get into it. The old man scurried down low, like a rat, and slipped inside. I followed him. Some rocks slipped off the edge when I came in and I heard them rattling on the rocks down where the sea was

throwing white stuff halfway up the cliff.

Inside the cave there was a shrine like you see all over New Mexico: The Virgin of Guadalupe. She was painted white and blue, the color of her robes, and she had very red lips. Her skin was as dark as the old man's, almost black.

I watched in silence as he deposited a leather bag at her feet, then he nodded we should go — and back up over those mean slippery little rocks and out over the cliff-edge. We walked back to the trailer, saying nothing. But, for once, I wanted to talk.

I asked him his name.

He was walking ahead of me on the beach, kind of hunching along in that wornout tweed coat, with the collar up against the wind, and he turned and said: "Hernando Cortez."

"Mine's Ponce de Leon," I told him.

He shrugged. But I had a hard time keeping up with him, he was such a fast walker, and I think I heard him laughing as he ducked around the surf a couple times.

Back in the trailer that night, he leaned back in the kerosene light that made his head seem bigger than it was, and said: "You find her all over Mexico. She is everywhere. She is everything."

"We have her too," I added.

He frowned."You do not see her in your heart," he said, "only with your eyes."

I don't know why… maybe it was my aunt, growing up the way I did, being Pueblo, but I started to cry. The tears came down my cheeks, burning hot, and I made no move to brush them off.

The old man paid no attention.

The kerosene light danced, the flame fought, briefly, with a desert moth. A sputtering sound of wings being consumed in flame. It was all I needed: that image hung before my eyes. The old man put a scalding cup of sheepherder's coffee into my hands. It burned them, but I did not flinch. He'd put an egg-shell in the pot, and mixed the day-old grounds with egg white. The coffee tasted like the desert, dry, despite its being wet.

After a while, he crawled off onto his cot, but before he closed his eyes he said to me:

"Down in the desert, up in the mountain... she is everywhere, my son."

Tears were still running down my cheeks.

"—And if I promise to see her with my heart—" I said drily.

"You can't," he cut back, "you can't do it."

"I mean, if I try—"

He laughed then, a hoarse cackle-laugh.

"There's no need to try," he said softly, earnestly. "You see, my son, she is our Mother. She is the reason I am alive and…."

He paused and I heard the soughing of the sea on the sand.

"—And you're not dead," he finished.

In another moment, his snores drowned out the sound of the surf.

I didn't sleep a wink that night. I lay awake, thinking. Towards dawn, when the sky began to turn a rosy light, I went outside and saw something. I was standing behind the trailer, smoking a cigarette, watching the clothsline swing in the sea-wind, when suddenly a saguaro cactus burst into flame. The green wands, the limbs of that odd, old desert tree began to burn. The flames ate up the tree, leaping from branch to branch. Slowly, as I watched, each branch guttered out as the fire tasted the watery element of the plant. In the end, only one finger of flame remained, and it stayed lit for a long time.

The sun rose clear that morning. The cormorants were dive-bombing the bay the way they always do. The old man got up, pissed, sighed with satisfaction, and put some beans on the fire to boil. I was looking out to sea when I saw the island, as if for the first time.

The old man saw me staring out to sea.

"Tiburon," he said, going back into the trailer to get the coffee pot.

"Island of the shark," I mused.

He came back out, banging the pot against his knee to get the old grounds out.

"It isn't ours anymore," he groaned, "used to be Seri, not anymore."

"Who owns it?"

"Mexican government owns it." He put the battered can on the crackling mesquite coals, stirring them with the shoe he held in his right hand. He was barefoot, still getting dressed, and mumbling to himself.

I kept staring at the island. It was the very direction the cactus had pointed when the big branch crumpled. It had just hung there like a burned invalid's black arm, smoking and pointing at the western sky. So I knew there was something there. Something I had to see for myself.

The old man, though he didn't say, had some idea what I was thinking. After coffee, he said, almost as if he were talking to himself:

"Friend of mine has a boat, goes to Tiburon."

It was agreed then, with a quick look in the eyes.

Several days later, the friend with the boat came by. It was a motorboat, not made — I didn't think — for the high seas, but I suppose I was mistaken, because he revved it up and we roared out into the bay, skipping across the waves like a coin.

Once we got there, I wondered what I was doing there. The island was a hard place sticking out in the sun. There was a cobble beach with a dead porpoise on it that smelled pretty awful. The old man and his friend, another silent Seri, sat in the boat on the cobble-rocks and smoked cigarettes, occasionally laughing at something that was said in soft whispery tones. The day was hot and bright, the sun sharp as glass. I ached to get into the shade, but there was none.

Finally, up the beach, I found a small canyon made by run-off from the hill above, and went into it. The walls were steep and wet from spillage. I tasted a drop on my tongue — even the fresh was salt on Shark Island.

What was I doing?

The vision… so what….. But the vision….

In the cool quiet of the slim canyon, I lit a cigarette, sat on a wet stone, began to think. The utter disorder of my life seemed, in that escape from the sun, a finely carved design, like one of the old man's wooden birds.

Inhaling deeply, I took off my shoes.

The cigarette smoke lingered in the close walls, curving upward.

I pressed my toes into the sand.

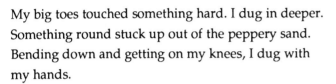

My big toes touched something hard. I dug in deeper. Something round stuck up out of the peppery sand. Bending down and getting on my knees, I dug with my hands.

A couple minutes later, I put it into my right pocket, put my shoes on, and went back to the waiting boat and the two funny old men, whispering and coughing and laughing in Seri, a language I did not know.

Some days later, I knew it was time to leave. I bid Hernando Cortez goodbye, thanking him for his hospitality. He said, "Be good to yourself, Ponce." That was all he said.

I walked back into Kino and ate lunch at a snack bar. He'd given me a small leather bag, just like the one he left in the cave. As I ate my tamale lunch, I fingered the drawstring of the bag. It was beaded: red, white, yellow, and blue. I could feel the cold beads on my fingers. In my other pocket was the gift from the sea that I would put into the bag when I got home to the Pueblo. There was a cave there, too. I could see myself going into it.

Hernando would be with me.

On December 9, 1531, the Virgin Mother of the Americas was first seen by a Nahuatl man on a hill outside Mexico City. The man saw at once that she was a vision, an answered prayer, an apparition of goodness.

"What do you want?" he asked humbly.

The Virgin of Guadalupe said, "I want you to tell the Bishop that I have come and that a temple should be built here, so that I can watch over my children for all time."

"Am I your child?" he asked.

She answered, "I am the Mother and you are the Child."

Book Two: CHILDREN OF THE MOUNTAIN

BEYOND BALD MOUNTAIN

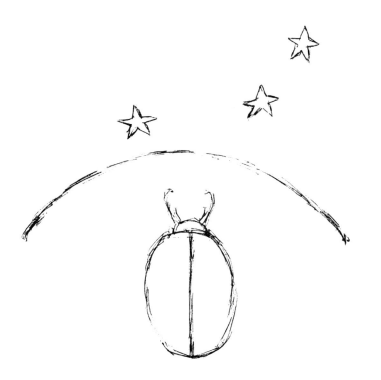

In the southeast, in North Carolina, the Cherokees still honor the mountain which has no trees on top of it. The story of the treeless mountain, now called Bald Mountain, goes back to the Cherokee creation story of how the world was made. Once, so the people say, the earth was one big floating island, suspended at the four-corners by deerskin thongs. Before that, however, there was no earth at all. The great sea, empty and wide, yawned into eternity. The Star People lived in the above-world in the dome of the sky. They were curious about what went on below, but they had no experience with it. So they sent Water Beetle down to explore. He went down to the the great sea, but there was nothing there. He went down to the bottom of the great sea, and there he found a foothold in some mud. Coming back to the surface, the mud came with him, stuck to his back. That is how the Cherokees say their world began.

Perhaps, when I was born, my grandmother, a thin leathery old woman known by many to be a witch, was the midwife.

She stood behind my mother and held up her arms while my mother kneeled on the floor. The medicine man gave her a decoction of the bark of the slippery elm to make the birth easier, after which he examined his beads to determine the future of the child.

Perhaps, as twins, we were not raised to be normal children, but witches. For twenty-four days we were secluded from all visitors and denied mother's milk. We were fed *connahaynee* corn, parboiled, beaten with a mortar and pestle, returned to the pot, boiled with beans, and kept in a large earthen jar.

And at the end of twenty-four days, my mother drank a decoction of the bark of the smooth sumac to make her milk flow abundantly, and then we were given the breast, confirmed as witches.

But something went wrong, because my brother is dead, and whatever else I can do, I cannot fly through the air tunnel through the ground, prepare and spoil food without touching it, divine others' thoughts, or walk upon sunbeams.

I have wondered about my twin brother, the other half of the burden of the womb.... what kind he was, what he might have been... they say he was fond of our grandmother and she of him... that he used to pick up things — pretty stones, a flower, even a dead bird, and bring them to her. Perhaps I dominated the breast and he felt left out.

Perhaps, like Snake Boy, my brother left the cabin one morning without breakfast, went into the wood, and was gone all day. Perhaps he returned in the evening with a pair of deer horns and went to a hut where his grandmother was waiting for him. Then he told her he must be alone all night. She left, but at daybreak returned and found an immense green serpent with horns on its head and human legs instead of a tail.

It spoke to her, told her to leave and she went away. When the sun was well up, it began to crawl out. It made a terrible hissing noise, striking through the air like a vibrant wind. The people fled as it crawled through the cabins, leaving a broad trail behind it, until it came to the river, a deep bend in the river. It plunged in, went under the water, and was never seen again.

Perhaps the grandmother, who was a witch, and who grieved over her grandson, also went down to the river and plunged in, and perhaps she saw him again. One day a man who was fishing saw the grandmother sitting on a large rock in the river, looking as she had always looked. But when she caught sight of him, she jumped into the water where Snake Boy, her grandson, had plunged, and she was gone.

As a boy, I watched hands dig clay from the bank of that same river, saw it fired in the open, smoked with crushed corn cobs, molded by hand, and decorated with paddles polished with smooth stones into pottery of chestnut-burr: frog, fish, bird or man. We wore, then, beads, pendants, ear-ornaments, and gorgets of animal teeth, of bird bone, of stone, of pearls from the mussel, of copper traded from the people, or from the great eastern ocean.

With my father I made arrowheads and spearheads of flint and of the antler of the deer. We made bows of locust and strings of the entrails of the bear; blowguns of bamboo; pipes of steatite and awls of bone. We gathered horse chestnuts and roots, pounded them into a powder, spread the powder over a lake or pond, stirred it with a pole until the fish — drugged by the powder — floated to the surface and were gathered in baskets. These were always covered to protect them from the moon.

Called to the village in late fall or winter, I would set out for the mountains. This, when I was much older. A vigil of prayer and fasting for four days, then I would hunt

and kill a deer. I would place the body in an exposed position, conceal myself, and sing the eagle-song in a soft under-breath way.

When the eagle appeared, I would shoot it. Then I emerged from concealment and stood over it, saying the eagle-prayer, asserting that it was not a Cherokee who killed it, but rather a Spaniard! Thus I averted the vengeance of the eagle spirits. I would leave the bird, return to the village, announcing that a snowbird had fallen thus, again, to mislead the eagles.

Four days later, when the beetles had deserted the eagle, we would go into the mountains, strip the feathers, and wrap them in a fresh deer skin. Then we would leave the body of the deer for the eagles and return to the village.

The feathers were hung in a small hut by the dance ground, a dish of deer meat and corn set before them to satisfy their northern tribes, of marine shells traded from the gulf, also the body of a scarlet tanager. The eagle dance was held that night and the eagle chiefs would wear the feathers.

Perhaps, I am dreaming.

If I dream of birds, I will go insane. If I dream of wrestling with a fat woman or having sex with my mother, I will be stricken with rheumatism. If I dream of bees and wasps, I will go blind. If I dream or have a vision of the the Darkening Land of the West, I will die.

Perhaps, then, I will no longer be a Cherokee... what does the name mean? People Who Live In Caves. The original word is *Chalaque*, the word used by the Choctaws, the people of the gulf coast who met DeSoto in Florida and who told him of us. Chalaque, the people who come out of caves.

Perhaps, if I stay in the cave that we came out of, they will not see me, hear me... I bear the wound of the rock in my shoulder, the tears of my mother in my heart.

Perhaps, at last, I should leave with the others, cross the highest ridge, the divide between east and west, cross and descend westward, follow our half-blood brother, Sequoyah, who tamed the wild animal of language, who wrote the word, who crossed the Great River.

— And went west, went west.

Perhaps to stay in the lake of Atagahi, which no man has ever seen, only animals. You will know it by the sound of wings: a thousand wild ducks and pigeons. Pray and fast and watch through the night. Floating lilies grow in its purple waters, fed by springs spouting from the high cliffs around it.

Atagahi, the medicine lake.

When a bear is wounded by hunters, he makes his way through the woods to the lake and plunges in. When he comes out upon the other side, the wounds are healed. But the lake is invisible to hunters, no man has ever seen it.

Turning from the lake and mountains, I enter the woods and cross the ridge, moving west.

Between 1832 and 1834, the Cherokee were driven from their homeland. As historian Oliver La Farge has said: "...by bribery, by persuasion, by fraud, and above all, by brutal force, the Indians of the Five Tribes were driven out of their homelands and moved to Oklahoma, a far, strange, unfriendly land." The rest of the story, recorded as The Trail of Tears, is infamous. Thousands died on the long march to their new home. Some were bayoneted trying to defend what was theirs, others saw white families moving into their homes as they were being driven away from them.

Of the fourteen to seventeen thousand Cherokees who traveled the Trail of Tears, some four thousand died on the way. The cost of their removal by the government was charged against the funds owed them for the sale of their lands. They arrived, therefore, already destitute. But the President of the United States was pleased. In 1838, he informed Congress: "...The Cherokees have emigrated without any apparent reluctance." Certainly, not all of the people were driven away.

Some, like the Navajos a century later, hid out in caves and secreted themselves in the forests of their homeland. Those who stayed knew what was theirs by birthright: for they had been there since Water Beetle dropped out of the sky. But not all those who stayed would stay for long. The cries of their brothers and sisters could be heard in their dreams, far into the 20th century.

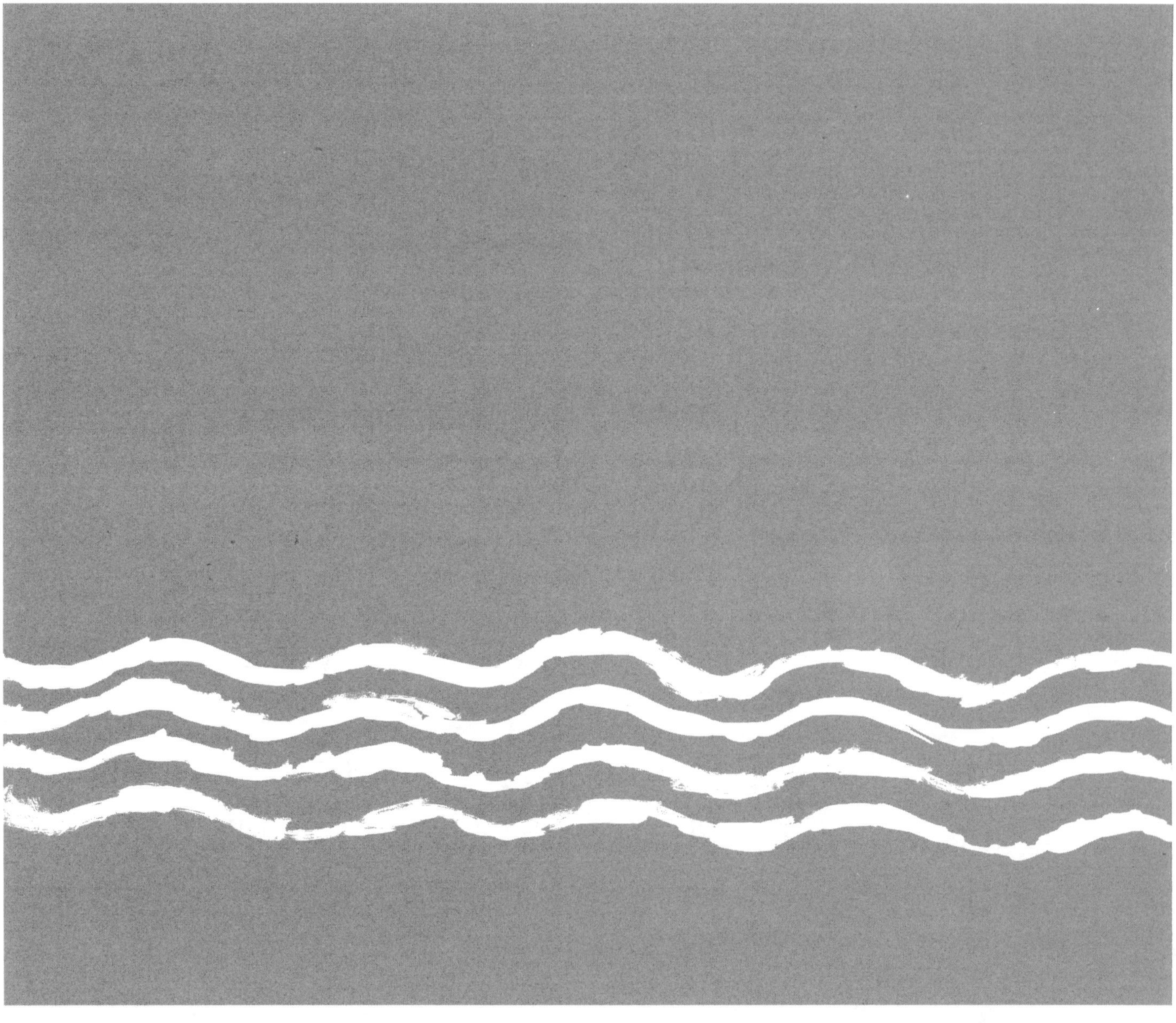

Book Three: CHILDREN OF THE WATER

BROTHER, LISTEN TO ME

In the 18th century, the sacred homeland of the American Indian was swallowed up by settlers from Europe. Treaty after treaty was made and broken. In fact, from the Indians' point of view, most treaties were made to be broken. The tribes of the eastern woodlands were pushed west, while the tribes of the west coast were exterminated altogether. Homeless and broken-hearted, many tribes that arrived in what was then called Indian Territory or the Indian Nations, the great reservation conceded to them, were absorbed by larger tribes. It is a bitter irony that some of the first tribes to befriend the white man were also the first ones to become extinct.

Another near-irony is that many of the chiefs, who spoke in council to their people, counseled not war but peace. Even when speaking of the loss of their land, they talked in tones of visionary eloquence. As the trials were endured, the orators spoke with angelic tongues, praising peace and condemning war. During a time when they might have resorted to deeds of violence, wise chieftains and medicine people spoke of compassion.

Yet even as they spoke, the boundaries determined as rightfully theirs by their forefathers were being swiftly erased. Again and again, their homelands got smaller and smaller, until, in the end, the treaties signed by the governing fathers of the original colonies meant, as the saying is, less than the paper they were printed on.

The dreams and visions that follow here were the last hope of an orphaned people. In reaching out, they prayed, one final time, to turn hate into love. These prayers sent out from the hearts of the Native American elders arrived in the hands — or, in most cases — upon the ears of English royalty and American statespeople. In one instance, the words were presented in person to George Washington. All of the speeches were delivered during the 18th and early 19th centuries.

If the Great Spirit were listening, the orators seemed to feel, so then might their brother, the white man. These, then, are the pleas of the people of Turtle Island America, asking only that those who listened might also hear.

UPON OUR OWN LANDS

Brother, listen to me: The first white people to come to this land were the French. When they came into these lakes, they brought presents and promises of peace. We took them by the hand, we embraced their father, the King of France, as our father.

Then came the people with red coats, the English: They said to us — "We will clothe you in the same manner as the French." But no sooner had they taken over our country, than another people, those with white clothes, drove the English from this land. We, again, took these people by the hand.

I have not come here on a begging journey. We live in a great way in the woods, and never see white people except in the Fall when the traders come. We have never begged, nor will we begin now. We only ask what is fair: to live independently upon our own lands.

> Spoken by the Chief of the Ottawas,
> Keewtagoushkum, at the Treaty of Chicago

The Ottawas were an Algonquian tribe living at the top of the Great Lake region in what is today Canada. Yet historically they made their way into Wisconsin, northeastern Illinois, Ohio, and Pennsylvania. A small part of the tribe, refusing to submit to the United States government, remained in Canada.

WHO IS LEFT?

Did any white man ever enter Logan's cabin and leave hungry? Did he ever come, cold and naked, and leave unclothed?

During the last long war, Logan stayed in his cabin, an advocate of peace.

When my countrymen passed me by, walking toward war, they said: "See, there is Logan, a friend of the white man."

Last Spring, in cold blood, my family was murdered all of them. Today there runs not a drop of my blood in any person.

I sought revenge, I found it. I now rejoice in the sunbeams of peace.

But who is left to mourn for Logan?

> Spoken by the Mingo Chief Logan
> to Lord Dunmore, the Governor of Virginia,
> sometime around 1774.

The Mingo people were a band of Iroquois who left their main village sometime before 1750. They gradually moved down the Ohio River, crossing the headwaters of the Scioto and Sandusky Rivers, where they became known as the Senecas of Sandusky. In 1800, they were joined by part of the Cayuga, who had sold out all their land in New York.

OLD AGE

I do not talk your language.

I can neither hear, nor make myself heard.

When I walk through your streets,
I see people busy at their work,
making shoes, hats, selling cloth.
I say to myself — which of these can you do?

And I answer: not one.

I can make a bow, an arrow, catch fish, kill game.
But none of these is of use in your city.
Old age comes and I must be in my own country.

      Spoken by Chief Little Turtle
      of the Miami tribe.

*This was his explanation of why he did not wish to live in Philadelphia,
but instead preferred to live on the banks of the Wabash River. The
Miami Indians were known as "the people who live on the peninsula."
They were first met by the French explorer Perrot in 1668, when they
were living along the Fox River in Wisconsin, but later they settled at
the south end of Lake Michigan and on the Kalamazoo River. Little
Turtle once said: "My fathers kindled the first fire at Detroit."*

LISTEN TO WHAT WE SAY

Brother, listen to me. It was the will of the Great Spirit that we should meet this day. He orders all things. He has taken his garment from before the sun and caused it to shine brightness upon us. Our eyes are opened: we see clearly. Our ears are unstopped: we hear well. For these favors, we thank the Great Spirit, and him only.

Brother, listen to what we say. There was a time when our forefathers owned this great land. Their seats extended from the rising to the setting sun. The Great Spirit made the buffalo, the deer for food. He made the bear and the beaver for clothing. He scattered them over the country and taught us how to take them. He caused the earth to make corn for bread. All this He did for His red children because He loves them. If we ever fought among our brothers for hunting grounds, these wounds were healed without the shedding of much blood.

But one day evil came upon us. Your forefathers crossed the great waters and landed on this island. Your numbers were small. They told us they had fled from wicked men and came here to enjoy their religion. They asked for a small seat, we gave it to them and they sat among us.

Then more of you came among us. We did not fear them. They called us brothers, we believed them, and we gave them a larger seat. Soon your numbers increased, you wanted more land, more country. Our eyes opened, our minds became uneasy. War broke out. For you, Indian fought against Indian. You brought strong liquor to us; many were killed from this; thousands more were slain. Brother, our seats were once large and yours were very small. Now you have become a great people and we have nowhere to spread our blanket. And now, brother, you have come to tell us that you are here to show us the proper way to speak to the Great Spirit. You say that if we do not listen to what you teach, we will be unhappy. You say that you are right and we are lost. Yet brother, your religion is written in a book. If it was intended for us to hear the Great Spirit in this way, why did He not also give us this book? And brother, if as you say, there is but one religion, then why do you fight so among yourselves over it? Why do you not all agree?

Brother, we also have a religion that was given to us by our forefathers and has been handed down to us, their children. Our religion teaches us to be thankful for all that we receive, to love each other, to be united.

Brother, we do not quarrel about religion.

The Great Spirit has made us all, but he has made us differently. For you he has given the arts. For us he has not yet opened our eyes to these things. He knows what is best for his children. Brother, we do not wish to destroy your religion or take it from you. We wish only to enjoy our own.

> Spoken by Red Jacket, the Seneca Chief,
> in answer to a missionary.

The Seneca, part of the Iroquois Nation, were known originally as "people of the rocks." They lived around what is now Seneca Lake and the Geneva River in northwestern New York. Red Jacket was one of the great Iroquois orators, who, after the Revolutionary War, during which he fought against the Americans, urged his people to return to the old ways. Unfortunately, he ended his own life as an alcoholic.

THIRTEEN FIRES

Father, when you kindled your thirteen fires separately, the wise men assembled there told us you were all brothers. They said you were the children of one great father who regarded the red people as his children. We were told he resided beyond the great water where the sun first rises. They said his goodness was as bright as the sun. What they said went into our hearts. We promised to obey him.

Then, when you refused to obey him, he commanded us to assist him in making you obedient. In obeying him, we were deceived, we drew closer to your fire and talked of peace, and made haste towards it.

But you said you could crush us to nothing. You demanded from us our country as the price of peace, as if our want of strength had diminished our rights. Our chiefs felt your power and gave up our country to you. What they agreed has bound our nation. But now at last, your anger by this time must be cooled, and although our strength is not increased and your power has not become less, we ask of you now, were the terms dictated to us resonable and just?

Spoken by Cornplanter, a Seneca Chief
to George Washington

Cornplanter was the principal leader of the Iroquois in their warfare against the Americans during the Revolutionalry war. The result of this speech was a peace treaty signed by the first President of the United States under which the Iroquois received reservations and became subject to the new nation.

SHALL WE GIVE IT UP?

A long time has passed since we first came here. Our old people have all sunk into their graves. They had sense. We are young and foolish. We fear to offend their spirit, if we sell our land. We fear to offend you, if we do not.

Our country was given to us by the Great Spirit to hunt upon and make cornfields, to live upon and make beds upon when it comes our time to die. The Great Spirit would never forgive us should we bargain our land away.

When you first spoke, we said we had little. We agreed to sell you a piece, but we said we could spare no more. Now you ask again.

I am an Indian, a red skin. I live by hunting and fishing, but my country is already too small. I do not know how to bring up my children, if I give it all away.

You are acquainted with the country we live in. Shall we give it up? It is a small piece of land, if we give it away, what shall become of us?

> Spoken by Metea,
> Chief of the Potawatomi people.

Metea was a famous chief, active in the Council of Chicago, where this speech was given. The Potawatomis lived between the great Lakes in what is now Michigan. From the French they obtained trade goods and arms, which enabled them to push other tribes out of their rich forested hunting lands. Among others they forced the Sioux westward, toward the Great Plains, the results of which transformed the tribe into the horsemen of the prairie.

FAREWELL

I have fought hard, but your guns were well-aimed. The bullets flew like birds in the air. They whizzed by our ears like the wind in the trees of winter. My warriors fell around me. It began to look dismal, I saw an evil day at hand.

In the morning, I saw the sun rise dim in the sky. In the night, it sank in a dark cloud. A ball of fire was the last sun that sank on Black Hawk. Now his heart is dead. He is a prisoner of the white man. But he has done nothing for which he is ashamed.

He has fought for his countrymen, for the squaws and papooses. He has fought for their land. Farewell, my nation. Black Hawk tried to save you and avenge your wrongs. Now he is taken prisoner and his plans are stopped. He can do no more. His sun is setting and he will rise no more. Farewell, Black Hawk.

Black Hawk, Chief of the Sauk and Fox tribe

Black Hawk fought for his homeland in what became known as Black Hawk's War. But even before the fighting broke out, his people had already been seriously weakened by treaties signed in whiskey, pledged in drunkenness. After his surrender, Black Hawk was confined to Fortress Monroe in Virginia; from there he was "paraded on tour" through the principal eastern cities, "proving to be an object of great interest." He died in Des Moines, Iowa, in 1838. In 1839, his body was stolen from its grave and taken to St. Louis. Eventually, Black Hawk's bones resided in the Burlington Geological and Historical Society where they were destroyed in 1855, when the building burned to the ground.

Book Four: CHILDREN OF THE GRASS

THE MESSENGER

The rumor of a new religion spread in all the cardinal directions, and it is said that only the Navajos and Pueblos — with the exception of Taos — did not take the news and act upon it. The word was that an "Indian Jesus" was alive upon the land, and that his preaching would save the Indian nations and bring back the great herds of buffalo. The people of the grass country were especially hungry for this news, for with the wholesale slaughter of the buffalo, they were without food. Here was a religion that promised them dignity and freedom from suffering; here was a chance to dance back the buffalo and turn the white man away from sacred ground. Here was a way to get back what they had lost, to turn back time and take out vengeance upon the stealers of their grasslands. Soon, they were told by messengers from the north, soon the Messiah would come.

In 1881, in the grasslands of Oklahoma, there came a man whose name was Red Robe. He was Arapaho and he had come down from the north on a mission of holiness.

If looks could kill, then Red Robe was a killer.

Everyone who saw him was convinced of his power. Fixing his tipi at the top of a little rise over the river, he held council, and most of the young men listened to him.

"The time is at hand," Red Robe said, "when the whites will be removed and the buffalo will again return."

"Where will the whites go?" a young man asked. Red Robe replied, "They will fade away."

"What will happen to the Agency set up by the whites to govern us?" a man asked.

"Fire will rain down from heaven and burn it up," Red Robe said.

"The soldiers will be angry with us then."

"Their bullets," Red Robe explained, "will have no effect upon the true believers."

Then Red Robe unwrapped a medicine bundle, which had in it a calendar known to the Kiowa. On white buffalo skin there was a painting of a tipi. A hail of bullets had stopped right in front of it. Guarding the doorway of the tipi was a giant buffalo.

Red Robe stayed with the Kiowa for one year, living a little apart from them, but teaching them of the new way, which he called the Ghost Dance. All during that year he made songs and prayers of buffalo medicine. But that year the buffalo did not return, and at the end of that year, Red Robe died of an unexplained illness. He was buried in his red robe with eagle feathers all around it.

I remember Black Coyote. He rose up among our people, the Kiowa, because he had a startling vision. We listened to him. On his chest and arms he had seventy scars.

"How did you get so many scars?" I once asked him.

My children died, as you know," he answered. "One after the other. During that time I did not eat for four days. And then I heard a voice. It was the cry of an owl or the low bark of a dog. Then it said to me: 'You will cut out seventy pieces of skin and give them to the Sun.' But I did not do as the voice said. I cut only seven pieces. These I held to the Sun, prayed over, and buried, as is our custom."

Soon after a dream came to me. In this dream the Sun Himself appeared before me. The Sun said: 'You will cut seventy pieces, and with each you will say a prayer for my family. Then you will bury the skin. If you do this, the rest of your own family will live.'

"I did what the Sun asked, and none of my family have died."

I listened to Black Coyote. Who did not? He was a powerful man. He would sit very straight and show his scars. We saw that he spoke the truth.

The year was 1890. That year the Arapaho prophet, Sitting Bull, came down to the grassy plains to talk to us. There was a great gathering from the north. Altogether we were Cheyenne, Arapaho, Caddo, Wichita, Kiowa, and Apache. We remained together for about two weeks, dancing every night until the sun arose.

I remember one night when we were all gathered together. Sitting Bull said he had something to show us. He stepped into the center of the dancing circle. He walked up to an Arapaho woman, passing an eagle feather in front of her face. Then she fell down and was asleep. Then Sitting Bull passed among the people gath-

ered there, and one by one, he made them fall with his feather. And they lay asleep on the dancing ground, all of them stretched out with their eyes closed, as if asleep.

I was not one of them, so I saw this with my own eyes. Then, many hours later, each one woke up, slowly, stretching as from a deep sleep. I heard what the people said. They said they had gone on to the Spirit World where they had met their dear departed families and friends. In the Spirit World they hunted buffalo, as in other days, and they sported on their ponies and there was plenty to eat for all. After they woke up, they were sorry to have come back. The people made songs to sing about the good remembered ways with their families in the Spirit World.

Some time after the night Sitting Bull showed his medicine, Cheyenne and Arapaho land was asked for purchase by the whites. Left Hand, of the Arapaho, went to Sitting Bull for advice.

"What should we do?" he asked.

And Sitting Bull answered, "The people are hungry, sell the land to the whites. Soon the Messiah will come and return the land to you."

The Messiah, we learned later, was a Paiute priest named Wovoka. Some of the people had already been to visit him and they had returned with magpie feathers, which they said were an important part of the Ghost Dance. When the white traders heard about this, they imported crow feathers and sold them to the people, two for a quarter. I also heard that some of the people took the grass-money paid to them by the cattlemen and bought the sacred red paint from Wovoka's desert country to use in the dances.

It was around that time that I was given the name Messenger, because of something that happened. Like many other Kiowas, I began to have dreams and visions of the Spirit World. In one of these, I met four young women riding on horseback. I saw that their saddle-pouches were full of wild plums. One of the women offered me one, but I was afraid to eat it because I knew that this same woman had died a few years earlier.

I asked her if she knew any of my family, and she said she did. I was directed to a man who told me that next to his tipi were my relatives. As far as the eye could see there was tipi after tipi, like blades of grass they had sprung up. When I went into the tipi he pointed to, I saw at once that it was just as he had said: My family was all in there: Father, two brothers, and two sisters.

They were very happy to see me and did not ask how I had come to be there. Instead they offered me buffalo meat from a large kettle over the fire. They could see that I was afraid to eat it, and they urged me to smell the meat, saying that it was good and I would like it.

In time I became known for this vision, and for others that I had. And in time I was asked by the people to travel, myself, to the Messiah and hear his words. I traveled by way of the Union Pacific Railroad to Nevada. At the Agency at Pyramid Lake, I got a wagon ride to the upper end of the Mason Valley. Not long after, we came to the small house of Wovoka, but I was told there that I must wait, that he was sleeping. I went away and returned the following day and this time I was taken in to see him.

He was lying down on the floor of the cabin with a blanket covering his face. He was singing to himself. The room was bare and dusty. At last Wovoka stopped singing and removed the blanket from his head. He was a dark man with small pinched features. He did not smile or show in any way that he was pleased to see me, or to know that I had come such a long way to see him.

"What can I do for you?" the Messiah asked.

This I felt was a strange question. Did the Messiah not know the reason for the visit? Was he making a joke? sHis face was most serious.

"I would like to travel with you to the Spirit World," I said.

There is no Spirit World here," he said.

"I would like to see my little child who has departed from me," I told him. He stared at me.

"There are no spirit children here," he said, "look around, see for yourself."

In the small dark room he looked like a shadow. Hard times were upon the man, I felt. He did not look as happy and wise as my friends the Arapahos had said.

He looked tired. And when I looked at his palms, I did not see the marks they had told me about, the scars they called the crucifixion. Not seeing the scars, I felt a heaviness in my heart. Even Red Robe, who had gone away, had the scars of his conviction. Wovoka looked empty, like something the wind had run through.

"Are you truly the Messiah the people are talking about?" I asked.

"There is no other," Wovoka replied crossly. Then: "You tell your people to quit this business, give it up. Tell them I say to do this."

"Why should I do this?"

"I gave the Sioux the new dance. But they twist things and make trouble. More trouble will come. Tell your people."

Then with a wave of his hand and pulling his blanket over his head, he dismissed me as if I were a white man. I went home and talked to the people and told them of Wovoka's wish. But even before I saw their faces, I knew it was all over for us, and even though the dreams kept coming to me, they were no longer important.

The Ghost Dance Cult, as it has sometimes been called, began with the Paviotso, a branch of the Paiutes of Nevada. The man imputed to be its founder, Jack Wilson, better known as Wovoka, mixed Christian ethical ideals and prophecy with Native American rituals. Through their own visionary experience, Native American medicine men such as Sitting Bull sought the millenium and redemption for all Native American people. Unfortunately, the essentially peaceful doctrine of Wovoka and other mystics was, in fact, distorted by some of the Plains warrior societies. This frightened the white settlers. In the end, Sitting Bull was killed in his own home by Sioux police hired by the United States government. After Wounded Knee, the Ghost Dance faded. However, there are certain vestiges of it, according to historian Oliver La Farge, in dances of the Nevada Indians.

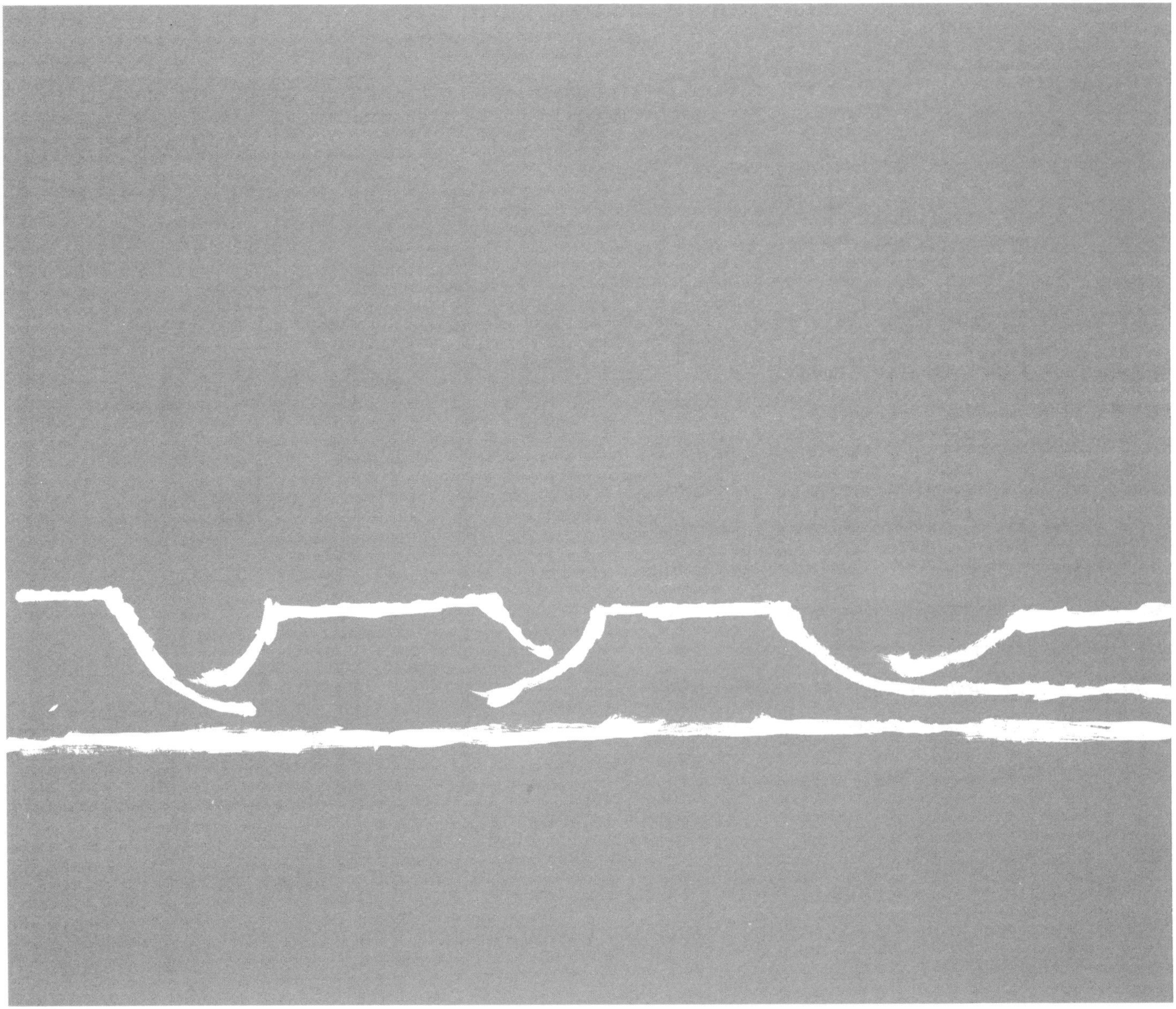

Book Five: CHILDREN OF THE MESA

DEER BOY

The Deer Dance, which is held in February at San Juan Pueblo in northern New Mexico, is a celebration, a vision, a dream, a dance, a myth, a communal event, a prayer, an act of love and faith. At dawn you can hear the ankle bells, and with the first light the coming of the "deer" off the mesa, where, half-clothed, they have been waiting all night long. The dance is for the benevolence of the animal spirits and the coming of spring with plenty of food for everyone. Once, according to legend, the dance was not done by people, but by the deer themselves. But the Deer Dance, like all things originating in myth, is beyond description, beyond measure. It brings man and animal into union, harmonizing the world of nature — "As it was in the beginning, so it ever shall be..."

Grandma used to tell the story
Of the boy who danced the deer dance so well
That at the end of the day,
He turned into a deer.

Sometimes, even now, people see the tracks
Down by the river.
Every year, when we do the deer dance
In February, we see the tracks.

They say, the old ones, that the spirit
Of the boy gets into all the dancers
When they dance — the old and the young
Dancing together.

When I danced the deer dance
For the first time, I was six years old.
I remember how it was: the bonfires up
On the mountain, just before dawn.

I was wearing my deer costume.
The horns that tie under the chin
And around the back of the head.
White kilt, white shirt.

The center of my face was red
With white clay
From the river
In a ring all around it.

And red clay on my hands and arms.
I was proud to be a young deer,
Waiting my turn to dance.
While we waited, down in the field,

Looking at the bonfires up on the mountain,
The singers were singing the deer songs.
Then, suddenly, just as the sky got pale,
We saw them coming.

They came out of the blue like a snowy cloud,
The deer dancers who had been out all night,
Alone, on the mountain. They were white
And they walked on their deer-sticks

The way deer do and as they came down
Closer to the village
All the women threw cornmeal
On them, and they prayed and touched them
On the shoulder. How beautiful the deer
Looked in their white sashes, their white
Shirts and kilts, with their bells

Ringing in the cold wintry air.
And the smell of evergreen was in the air
From the branches, saved since Christmas,
That the deer wore on their kilts.

I was proud to be a deer myself
And to join the dancers that day.
A long day it was, too.
First we danced through the village

In front of the church,
Then in the plaza.
Then we went into the kiva
Which is our ceremonial place.

I was not the youngest deer that day:
There was one three years younger,
And when I looked at the grandmothers —
Some of them in their eighties

I did not feel too young or too old.
But as the day wore on, I did grow tired
Dancing with my back straight
Four times towards the church

Four times towards the mountain
Four times towards the river
Four times towards the valley.
That was the way it was done.

All day it lasted, this dance of dances.
And when I got tired and my knees
Got shaky, old grandfather, dressed in bucksin,
With his otter-fur cloak

That had the pink shell in the middle
Of his chest
Came over to where I was standing
And danced very close to me.

He seemed to be saying, not in words
But the way he danced — so straight and tall
And strong — "If I can do it, you can too."
I remember that it was the power of his presence

That kept me going near the end of the day.
I would look at his beautiful bow
And his quiver of arrows
And the little downy eagle feather

Tied to his hair, and his feet keeping beat
With the drums, and this would give me strength.
Then, just before sundown, the deer dance
Came to a close.

That was the moment when all the watching
Women became excited.
— "Get back, get back —" the officials said.
But this made the women more excited.

The villagers and out of town people
Were everywhere — around the plaza, on the rooftops.
Then came the two Apaches, the ones who
Carry the little deer to different houses

So they will not get hurt in the stampede.
They pretend — these Apaches hunters — to shoot
The little deer and they pick us
Up and put us over their shoulders.

One of the Apaches has a big shotgun
And when he pulls the trigger, that is the
Signal the dance is over.
— Boom! goes the gun, and deer go everywhere:

To the river, to the hills, to the mountain
Where they started out. Girls are running
After them to catch them, for as everyone
Knows the deer must be captured before
The sun goes down.
My mother warned me to get caught
Before sundown
Because this was why The Boy turned into a deer.

But the deer do not let
Themselves be captured so easily.
They put up a fight, striking out with
Their deer-sticks.

The villagers try to get hold of the horns
And hold the deer in back of the head
So they will calm down
And be captured.

The little ones, of which I was one,
Do not have to fight to get free
For it is our fate to be sold off
To the village mothers

And be taken to their home.
I went away with a lady I did not know.
But it was alright because when
We got to her adobe house

It was warm inside with the glow of the
Woodstove, and there was the smell of juniper
Burning and chili cooking on the stove,
And I was so tired.

I remember that I sat down and ate.
There was chili stew, Indian bread,
And Coca-Cola. While I was eating,
The lady asked me my mother's name.

It is our custom to go home after we eat.
But I was so tired, I fell asleep
At the table with my hand around an apple.
My mother was going from house to house

Looking for me, and I was sound asleep
Having a dream. In the dream, I was running
By the river, singing the deer song.
The pretty girls were coming after me

But I just flicked my white fluff tail
At them and danced away. They could not
Catch me, I was too springy for them.
I ran and ran until I was at the top

Of the mountain, looking down on the
Village. Then I got scared — the sun
Was like a circle of fire on the mountain's
Rim, and no one had caught me yet.

Then I understood why — just as the sun set
And the air grew very cold.
It was dark by then and I knew that
I was the Boy Who Turned Into A Deer.

I walked into the darkness, alone.
I was a deer. There was nothing to do
But join the other deer down by the
River. In the dream I wondered if I

Would ever see my mother again.
My eyes filled with tears.
I began bucking and kicking, snorting
At the surrounding darkness.

Then I woke up and someone was holding me.
It was my mother, my real mother.
She carried me out to the car.
I had a big basket in my arms,

Given to me by the lady who had "bought" me.
In the basket were oranges and apples,
biscochitos, plums, bread, red chile, posole,
Pies, cakes.

In the car going home, my mother asked
"Why did you kick at me
When I tried to wake you?"
And I said, "I was having a dream."

Then she said, "I think it is time
For my little deer to go home —"
And I nodded sleepily, for I wanted
Nothing more than to fall into

My own bed and go to sleep, perhaps
To dream again —
To be The Boy Who Turned Into A Deer —
To dance on the hill

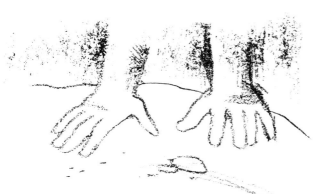

Then my uncle came and took me down
To the river to wash off the red and white
Clay. After that, I was a deer no more.
We buried my deer sticks by the river

Where they would stay until next year.
Then we went home
And the longest and best day of my life
Was finally over.

And run to the river
And watch all the girls try to catch me
And see them fall.
For no one could catch

The Boy
   Who
      Turned
           Into A Deer.

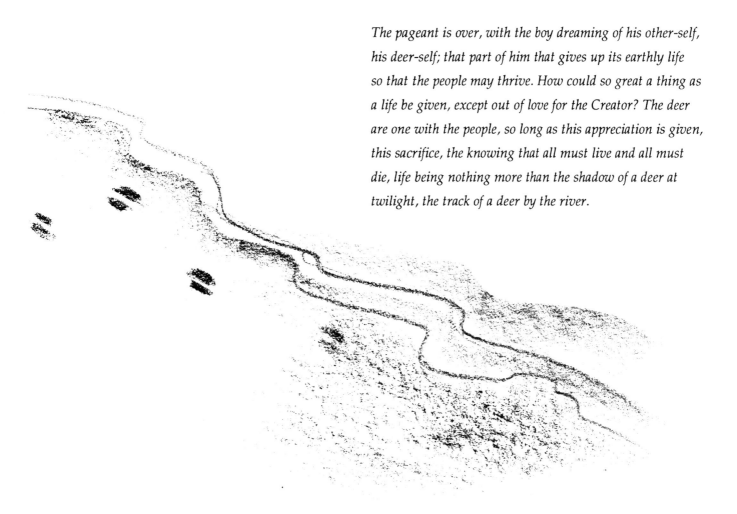

The pageant is over, with the boy dreaming of his other-self, his deer-self; that part of him that gives up its earthly life so that the people may thrive. How could so great a thing as a life be given, except out of love for the Creator? The deer are one with the people, so long as this appreciation is given, this sacrifice, the knowing that all must live and all must die, life being nothing more than the shadow of a deer at twilight, the track of a deer by the river.

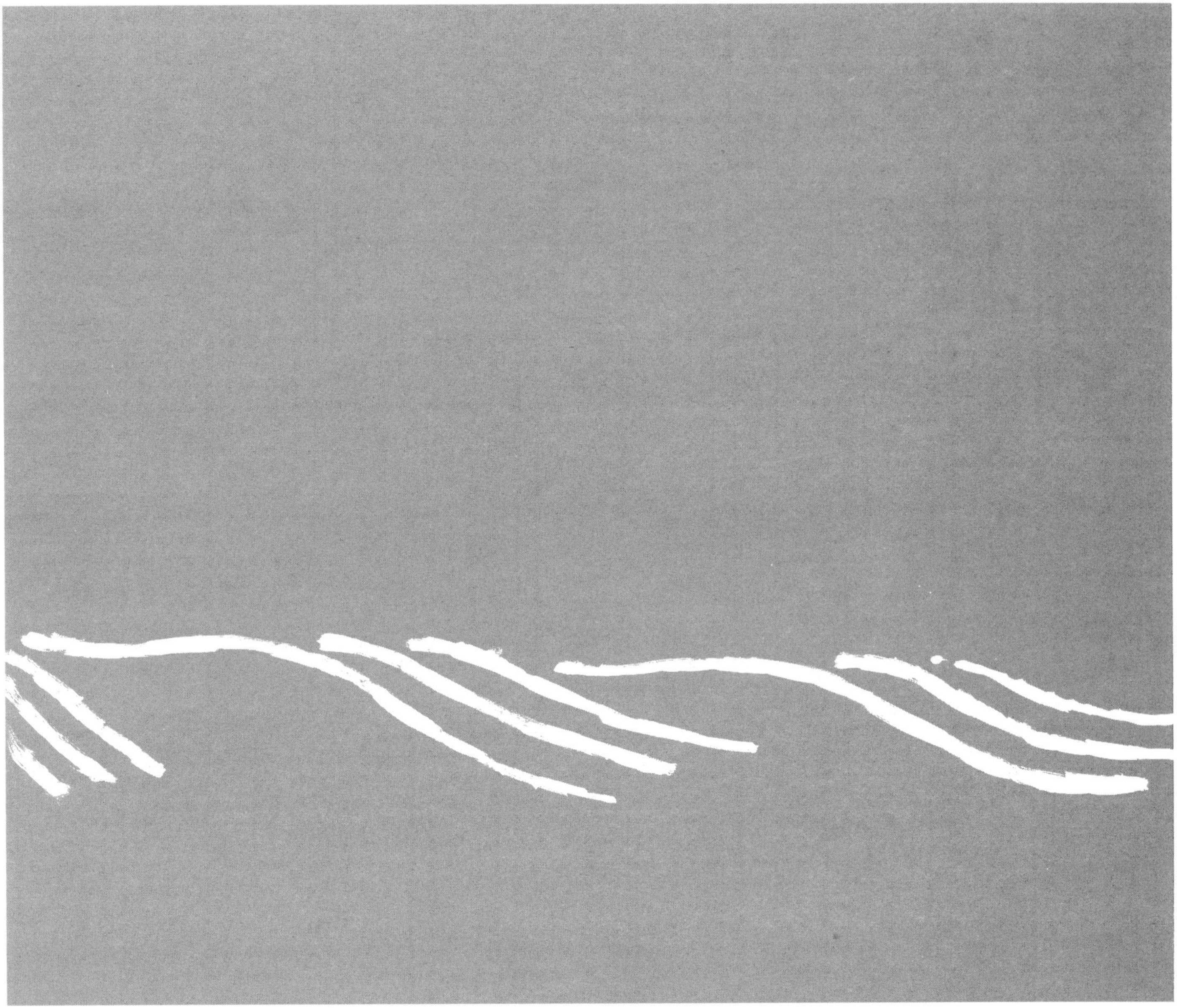

Book Six: CHILDREN OF THE SAND

THE SUN HORSE

In Navajoland it is said that the Sun Father rides across the sky, carrying the sun. He has five horses: a turquoise horse, a white shell horse, a pearl horse, a red shell horse, and a horse of coal. The different horses of the Sun Father reflect, in metaphorical terms, the temperament of the sky. The horses of the Sun Father are sacred. According to legend, he feeds them flower-blossoms and gives them sacred waters to drink. On his horse the Sun Father rides proudly across the sky, thus conferring upon the Navajo an image of greatness.

Riding his own mount, the Navajo rider returns, in ritual, the obeisance he feels for the Sun Father, the horse, the four directions. For all are holy, as is the man or woman who meditates upon them. Even the dust brought up by the wind of a clear summer day has its place of holiness. Navajos say that the mist on the horizon is the pollen of the gods.

*The story of the Sun Horse comes from my Navajo friend,
Jay de Groat, who has been telling stories to me since the
mid-sixties. In the telling of this one, a true story, he
describes the return of hozhoni — harmony — into the life
of a man educated in the white world.*

*A friend had told Jay: "You are without a horse; you
are not mobile," and though he had a degree from a
university, he lacked his own sense of Navajo self-esteem.*

*In returning to the Sun Horse, he gives himself back to
The People, and thus, back to himself.*

There was a place he knew.

A sacred butte, miles from his family's ranch. It was out there in the cedarland where The People did the Rain-praying Ceremony.

Rainy Butte.

Saddling the old horse given to him by his mother for the trip, he rode off in the direction of a dream, not knowing what he would find.

A piece of memory, maybe.

Twelve men had gone up Rainy Butte. Twelve men, a young boy, a young girl. The boy was himself, the girl, someone he knew. And the men were elders of the tribe.

Twelve men and two children. He was the water-carrier; she was the cornmeal-carrier. He carried the black water-jar and she carried the basket. And all the time they walked up Rainy Butte, the lead singer at the head of the line of men sang the songs of rain.

He remembered all of it. The night's wait in the tipi-hogan made of plants, the center poles made of trees. All night there was singing in the pinetree-sprucetree house, with the roots turned up to the sky. Before dawn, they left that place and went up Rainy Butte. He was Corn Boy, she was Corn Girl. And the twelve elders were like the twelve Yei, or Holy People. Up into the Navajo dawn they walked, solemnly, their footsteps like prayers.

At the top of Rainy Butte, he remembered, you could see Mount Taylor to the south; Mount Hesperus to the north; Mount Blanc to the east; the San Francisco Peaks to the west. If you could not see them, you could, if your heart was strong, feel them.

But all that had happened many years ago. What did he feel now as he rode to the foot of Rainy Butte? One thing his father had said, this time, before he left: "Do not be afraid of what you may see up there on top." That was all he had said. It was enough.

Above all he knew the rules to abide. Wait for the rising sun. Do not show fear. Expect nothing, keep an open mind, be still, face east. For as he well knew the gods did not often bless the wary, the fearful, the careless or the proud. They gave their blessings to the simple of heart, the strong of heart, those who could wait.

Until now his life had been a shambles. College had given, and taken. It had given him knowledge, but it had taken his soul. Now, riding into the valley of dreams, he saw himself redeemed. He saw his life take shape before his eyes. Riding the rough trail to Rainy Butte, he felt the light sprinkle of rain. For a while, the gentle needles tickled his face and wetted his horse. He rode on, thinking. Then the rain let up, the sun came out. The sky went aqua, a coppery green. The damp cedars burned green in the subterranean glow, and a short rainbow glittered the valley with slabs of primary light.

Suddenly, looking down in the glare, he saw them: tracks of the Sun Horse in the wet sand. Seeing the little winged shapes of the unshod horse reminded him of the story his father told, the legend of the Sun Horse, how it came to life.

When the Holy People first made the horse, it was a complete thing, but it would not come to life. They tried to get it to rise up on its strong legs, but it would not rise. Caterpillar was asked to help.

"How can I help?" he asked.

"You know," one of the Holy people said, "where the sacred flints are kept."

"Yes, this is true. But I am so slow getting around."

Then the Holy People prayed over Caterpillar and he became Butterfly. Swiftly he flew to the Mountain Where Flint Is Kept, and gathering four flints, he returned to the Holy People and put the flints into the hooves of the horse.

The great horse stirred, quivered, came to life. Then it surged, leaped into life, struck the air with its hooves, and galloped off into the clouds.

"Look," a Holy Person said, "the horse makes the marks of Butterfly when it dances on its hooves."

And, it has been that way ever since.

It rained all day, washing away the tracks of the horse. Tying his own horse to a cedar tree, he found a dry place for himself under the cliff-edge. Under the rock-overhang he made a fire and hung his wet clothes on cedar sticks to dry them out.

Night came on, the moon and rolling clouds passed over his head. Wrapped up in a warm blanket, his round-topped, flat-brimmed Stetson pulled down over his eyes, he hardly knew if he slept or remained awake. The wind came up and brought with it a spice-breath of wet sage. Wind, in the old stories, was always a messenger. Hidden under his hat, he wondered, now, if wind was trying to tell him something.

He felt a chill on the back of his neck.

There was a whispering that was not wind. Then he heard a voice, voices. One Spanish, one American. Different sounding ways of talking: one that slipped, soft; one that skimmed like a flat rock on a pond. Wind, the messenger, brought the voices to him now.

He got up from the fire, and stepping free of his blanket, put on the half-dry clothes. The jeans were stiff and damp, he pulled them stiffly on.

The men, he judged, were quite close to his camp. Stealthily, he crept up on the ridge, dodging the broad swaths of moonlight, when the moon came out of the clouds. Finally, when he gained the crest of the ridge, he saw them, the whisperers on the wind.

There was a lone cedar in the moon on the top of the ridge. An owl, sitting on a dead branch, was whispering to a coyote, sitting on moonlit haunches under the tree. Their voices came clearly to him as he lay on his belly, listening to them talk.

He did not wait around, but drew back silently, brushing his footprints with a cedar bough. When he got back to the campfire, he heaped dead wood on it, building the flames into a small bonfire that lapped at the edges of the rock cove where he had made his camp.

Then, crouching by the fire, his horse saddled and ready to ride, the reins in his hand, he waited out the night. Sometimes, restless dreams came after him, but he shook them off, staying awake. Warnings, like woodrats, scampered through the thoughtless bin of his brain —

he chased them out.

In the early hours before the dawn, he drifted off.

A voice said to him: "If a man counts out his days, he will die."

"I haven't done that," he said aloud.

The voice said: "If a man whistles in the dark, ghosts will haunt him."

"I never whistled."

"If you dream your horse is dead, you will die."

"I've chased away evil dreams."

"If someone pulls your teeth in a dream —"

"— I've had no dreams —"

He jumped to his feet. It was nearly dawn. Facing east, he rode into the chilly morning. As he rode away from the ridge, he thought he heard something tinkling musically in the air. Too cold for Hummingbird, he mused. He craned his neck, looked back at the lone cedar. The unholy pair were gone. But in the steely light of dawn, he saw a pair of ancient spurs twinkling silver on the fading moon. He shivered and rode on.

Riding into the first light of the sun, he said the morning prayer of *hozhoni*:

> May all be well above me
> May all be well below me
> May all be well all around me
> The sky, be well
> The earth, be well
> The light, the darkness
> The mystery that is fire
> The prayer that is water
> In harmony it is done
> In harmony it is finished
> May harmony be all around me
> All the days of my life

Memory brought it back: the old trail of childhood, up the foot of Rainy Butte. Tying his horse to a tree, he took it on foot. The climb was much harder than he remembered, though. His legs were older, less sure of themselves. As he climbed, he blessed his legs, his feet, his boots. And climbing, kept climbing.

What he found, he knew. The trail back into himself. The muddy old trail into forgotten places of the mind. The jagged rocks, the slippery jointed cracks, the slick cobble, the falling-off places.

At the top, in the dawn sun, he prayed again.

> I walk in plain sight of my home
> I am at the entrance of my home
> I am in the middle of my home
> I am at the back of my home
> I am on the top of the pollen footprint
> Before me it is beautiful
> Behind me it is beautiful
> Under me it is beautiful
> Above me it is beautiful
> All around me it is beautiful

He felt himself rising and expanding with the words of the prayer. He felt the world echo with this expansion. The brightness all around him turned brighter.

And something happened.

His father's words came back to him: "Don't be afraid of what you see up there."

The horse came suddenly out of the sun. A golden horse with a mane of sunrays, with feet of flint butterflies that clattered on the clouds. It came out of the sun and thundered upon the clouds, and kicked lightning loose on the world.

He trembled at the sight of it.

It came right at him, its nostrils flaring, an aura of pollen shining around its head, a song coming from its hooves, a dancing, wild, prancing, golden horse with a wildflower hanging from the corner of its mouth.

It galloped at him.

He closed his eyes, praying softly.

The horse was almost on him, he could feel its oncoming surge, the force of its body moving through the light of morning.

It will crush me, he thought, it will surely crush my bones to dust.

But his father's words returned to him, again and again, until he himself was repeating them like a chant.

Then he closed his eyes and the horse came on into the night of his head, a sunbeam in its mouth for a bridle. He wanted to dive under its terrible hooves, but he held to the vow of his father's words. Sucking his breath deep within the cave of his bones, he released his fear; he gave out a great shuddering of breath into the morning air. His shoulders fell, his head drooped.

And the horse of the sun passed lightly through him. He felt it enter him, go through him, go beyond him. He opened his eyes: the horse was going down the steep trail to the foot of Rainy Butte.

He saw the golden-white of its tail flick furiously as it danced down the rocky trail, a cloud of dust rising in its wake.

In the gentle rain that fell after it was gone, he sang the song of the Sun Father's horse.

Hear his whinny now —
The horse of heaven,
Sun Father's horse
See him feed on flowers now —
The horse of the Sun
Whose butterfly hooves
Dance upon a cloud
Watch him disappear now
Sun Father's horse
Into the mists of sacred pollen
Hidden, he is hidden
Hear, now, his neigh
Sparkling water falls from his face
Dust of glittering grains
Rises at his hooves
Hidden, he is hidden
Deep within us
The horse of heaven
The Sun Father's horse

The story of the horse of the sun was told to me, as I have mentioned earlier, by Jay de Groat. Twenty-five years ago, he told me the first part of it, saying that if I were patient, one day he would tell the rest. I waited. Finally, he told it. As he told it, I understood the horse, a wild palomino that lived near his ranch in Crownpoint, was both magical and real, myth and flesh.

This story is apocryphal in the sense that it explores the psyche of a man troubled by the two worlds he has been born into — the Navajo tribal world which is spiritually complex and the white world which is materially complex. Jay, as participant in both worlds, straddles them on the horse of dreams, the horse of visions. Using his Navajo faith, he becomes himself, he completes himself. The reason why it took him so long to tell the story, he explained, was that he had to wait until he knew the meaning of mobility; why the horse came to him and him alone. As he put it, "There is snow on the mountain, I can tell the story." The snow he referred to was "the white" in his hair. Also, the traditional time to tell Navajo stories is wintertime. We have waited, Jay and I, for the first old, long, new snow.

Book Seven: NAMES AND SYMBOLS

Native American Symbols and
Tribal Names in Sun Horse

Animal People The myths vary according to the tribe, but the Animal People are always foremost, primary characters on the first plane of life. In some cases, an animal appears as the Creator, or as one of the Creator's helpers. The Maidu legend describes a void with no "before" or "after." Out of this falls Silver Fox, the Creator, and Coyote, co-creator and chief antagonist. Thus, the world of the Maidu begins. Many Southwestern Indian legends tell of a world "down-under," a First World of ants, beetles, locusts, and animal people who "move up" into successive worlds and co-create the present world we live in now. The Animal People, along with a First Man and First Woman, are responsible for bringing order out of the chaos of the early stages of life on Earth. Most tribes agree that the animals of today are creature-representatives of the original Animal People, whose spirits still inform and guide them. In this sense, the first Animal People are deities, and their ancestral children, the animals around us now, are their spiritual offspring.

Apache The Apaches and the Navajos were once of the same tribe. Both were Athapascan nomads who came down from the cold country of the North. Eventually, the Navajos settled into the Four Corners region where they still live. The Apaches of former times moved about a great deal, being both a mountain and a desert people, and covering an expanse from Mexico to Texas and much of the great Southwest. Noted for their warrior nature, the Apaches were one of the last tribes in America to lay down arms and submit to the reservations designated by the White Man.

Arapaho One of the major tribes of the Algonquian family, the Arapaho lived in a territory ranging from the plains of Colorado to the mountains of Wyoming. The Arapahos, along with the Sioux, Cheyenne and Kiowa, adopted the Ghost Dance Religion. This included the Basin-type round dance, with women participating, that was new to the Plains people in the late 19th Century. The Ghost Dance Cult began as a result of Christian mission influence among the Paviotso, a branch of the Pahutes or Paiute of Nevada. Its founder, in the latter part of the 1880s was Wovoka, or Jack Wilson, who began his career by having visions. Preaching peace and forbidding fighting, Wovoka created rituals to bring back vanished game animals and tribesmen killed in battle, and to revitalize the old Native American way of life. Dancing back the buffalo and weaving ghost-dance shirts that were believed to be bulletproof appealed to the Plains tribes, whose need for "magic" came at a time when their numbers were shrinking due to the increasing depredations of White soldiers. Unfortunately for Wovoka, his message of peace was misunderstood by Indian and White alike. Whether Wovoka was all prophet or part charlatan, no one can truly say.

Bark   Northeastern Native American tribes used bark for a variety of purposes: medicine, dye, shelter, clothing and even as a food-source. An Algonquian tribe was known as Bark Eaters because, having no other food during the cold months, they subsisted on the nourishing skin that lay just under the surface of the bark. In this search for sustenance, they were not unlike the deer and other bark-eating herbivores.

Bead   Before glass beads were introduced by Europeans, Native Americans made beads from quill, shell, bone, horn and other natural things including seeds, nuts and roots. Strung together and made into wampum, beads became more than ornamental; they became a part of the economy and were used in trading.

Bear A duality symbol, the bear is both maternal and kind, male-rough and dangerous. By turns, it is also female-vengeful and male-powerful. Native American legends describe bear power as desirable as well as sometimes uncontrollable. Many rites and rituals make the bear into an ally who brings powerful medicine for healing. Bear power comes from the earth. Bear was once assigned by Mother Earth to watch over travelers, those who, like Bear, roam about looking for a place to live.

Beaver November, for some eastern tribes, was the time of the Beaver Moon, when the most work had to be done before winter. The beaver assumes the role of the workman in most Native American tales, and this image, naturally, was passed on to the first European settlers.

Buffalo To the Plains people, as well as many other tribes, the buffalo was not only a food source, but a sacred being. It was the symbol of leadership, metaphor of long life and abundance. When a buffalo was killed for food, shelter, and clothing, care was taken to use all of its parts — the hooves, the horns, the tallow and the marrow.

Butterfly Due to the natural beauty of its wings, Butterfly is often considered vain. Yet, in Navajo mythology, Butterfly brings the sacred flint to the hooves of the horse. In the legend of the deity, Butterfly Boy was cured of his vanity by being lightning-struck with the axe of Rain Boy. After that, his head opened up and out of it came the butterflies of this world. The damageable dust of Butterfly's wings is sometimes thought to prove that such beauty is usually not durable.

Caddo The Caddo was a confederacy of tribes visited by La Salle in 1687. They lived in what are now the states of Arkansas, Louisiana, and Texas.

Carib The Carib are an Amerindian tribe, originally from South America, who traveled into the Caribbean Islands and conquered the Arawaks. Often noted as warlike, the Caribs are also described in 19th Century history books as cannnibalistic. Today, members of the tribe still live on in a reservation on the Caribbean island of Dominica.

Caterpillar In Navajo belief, Caterpillar is sacred because of his ability to transform into Butterfly, the gatherer of the sacred flint. However, while Butterfly may not always be trusted because of his vanity, Caterpillar is a simple, many-footed walker through life. Like Worm, he may give advice to his "betters."

Cayuga The Cayuga were one of the five nations of the Iroquois, who originally lived along the shores of Cayuga Lake in New York.

Cedar This ancient tree is used for burning and ceremonials. Its berries have been used against many contagious diseases and the needles, made into ash and mixed with water, are used as a dye. Cedar smoke often smudges the air in Southwestern Indian ceremonies; the boughs are cut and made into ceremonial dwellings, places for chanting and healing, as well as for shade from the sun.

Cheyenne A member of the Algonquian family, this Plains tribe once lived in what is now Minnesota. Once farmers and pottery-makers, they became, like the Sioux, horsepeople of the plains, following the buffalo herds and living in tipis.

Choctaw The Choctaw are a Muskhogean tribe first visited by De Soto in 1540. They were mainly agriculturalists and fought, by and large, defensively.

Corn Boy, Corn Girl, Cornmeal Carrier Corn is the most sacred of all Native American plants. Originally, it came from native grasses of Mexico and Guatemala and was brought to Turtle Island by Mexican Indians and the Carib people. Standing straight and tall, corn resembles human beings standing in rows. White corn is thought, by the Navajo, to be male; yellow corn is female. Round-headed corn symbols are men; square-headed are female. Food made from corn — especially cornmeal — is symbolic of the goodness of Mother Earth and Father Sky. Corn pollen is used in many blessing ceremonies, as is cornmeal. Strings of hardened corn kernels are made into necklaces. Corn, as Jay de Groat has put it, is "Mother Earth's workmanship."

Cornplanter Cornplanter (c. 1732-1866) was a Seneca chief who was also known as John O'Bail, which was his White father's name.

Coyote Coyote is the inimitable trickster common to legend in most Native American tribes. Both sacred and profane, Coyote gives birth to mischief and promise, he is a deceiver, but also a deliverer of good. Through his actions, change becomes possible; and change, though good and bad, brings newness and breaks conformity.

Dawn The rising and setting of the sun are sacred times for Native Americans. The strength of the sun is believed to be at its most potent at sunrise. Therefore, prayers and offerings are made to the Sun Father at this time. Offerings of cornmeal follow the sun's path, going sunwise, in a circle from east, south, west and north. Navajos describe four colors of the dawn, including afterglow. Symbolically, dawn is the beginning of the world, first-light, the place the people have come from their previous worlds of darkness.

Deer Dance   The deer is one of the most sacred of all animals. To dance the deer dance and sing the deer song is to call forth the blessing of the deer. Many tribes believe that the animal people are representatives of the powerful deities that govern them. In the deer dance the deer are symbolically called and brought into the Pueblo. Through the dance, the deer become a part of the people's lives, and the people pray for their continuance. The dance may be seen as a prayer for deer, a prayer for all sentient life, a prayer for the eternal bounty of nature. It is thought that when a deer gives its breath — its spirit — to a hunter, then, and only then, may the hunter have its life. The little deer children in the dance are taken into the homes of the people and given food, warmth and kindness. Later, they are released to their rightful parents. This act of charity, of bringing the deer into the home, is a ceremony of propitiation and good spirit. When the hunter brings home the deer, he does so with its permission, asking it to participate in the lives of men.

Deer Sticks   The canes or wooden sticks held by the deer dancers resemble the forefeet of the deer. After the dance, the sticks are hidden safely away in a secret place, in nature.

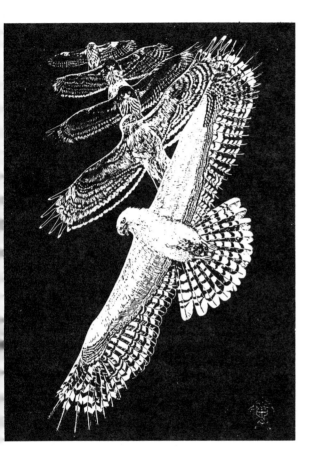

Feather As a common denominator the feather figures importantly in Native American myth, method and tribal practice. The feather is a metaphor for flight, a messenger to the spirit world. Feathers are used decoratively, as prayer symbols, and as designs of power. Attached to an arrow, the feather becomes the universal emblem of the hunt, of flight, of finding the mark.

Eagle Of all birds in Native American mythology, the eagle is the most important as symbol, sacrificial/ceremonial presence, and ultimate predator/warrior. The solitary mystery and power of the eagle as perceived by the Indian was immediately grasped by the emerging nation of the United States, and "borrowed" for its logo.

Five Civilized Tribes The Cherokees, Chickasaw, Choctaw, Creek, and Seminole were called the Five Civilized Tribes. In a sense, the name is not complimentary, for it was given because they, in the minds of their White neighbors, achieved a degree of civilization. These five tribes are really credited with donating their tribal organization to the first European settlers. Democracy came out of an understanding of the ways of these five tribal groups, and was adopted by the Whites rather than conferred by them to the Indians. In exchange for this, the democratic Euro-Americans took most of the land their former friends and neighbors lived on, and thus we have, among other things, the Trail of Tears.

Five Horses The five horses of the Sun Father are a way of telling time, Navajo-style. White shell and pearl horses represent dawn, turquoise is noon, red shell is sunset, and jet or coal is night. The fifth horse, according to legend, does not have a designated color

Four Times The number four is representative of the four directions, the four quarters, the four seasons, and the four worlds the people passed through getting from the underworld to this one, which some tribes say is the fifth world. Thus, many things are divided into fours, and the fourth time something is done, it always comes out the best.

Ghost Most tribal people believe in a spiritual resonance that lives after the life cycle is over. Native American myths describe this as a Spirit rather than a ghost. Spirits that reside in certain rock formations were once living, breathing beings. There are spirits in living trees which live on in the grain of the wood, or the smoke. Though in appearance a tree is "dead," it is yet "alive." Ancestor Spirits may live in inanimate objects, confined there, as it were, from previous existence. But in human terms, the Spirit of a man usually moves — unless hindered in some way — to one of several places. The Spirit World is often thought to be the one above this world. Yet it is also true, in some tribes, that the Spirit World exists underneath the one we live on now. In any case, Spirits do not come back to molest the living unless their pattern has been broken or disturbed, or unless they are compelled or directed to return. Many Native American "ghost stories" describe an individual whose Spirit leaves his body and goes to the Spirit World to join his departed family members in a place that corresponds with the Christian view of Heaven.

Great Flood Most tribes have a flood story similar to the one in the Bible. Water, in the legends, is a primary world, a pre-world; one that gives birth to the present one. Through the energy of water, man is forced or driven to rise to a higher plane. In many origin stories, the People are (as in the biblical tale) indifferent to their plight, and thus only the worthy, the "listeners," men, animals, birds and insects are brought up into the next world. The flood is a purifier which shows that the earth's creatures are somehow out of balance. In the Creek legend, the People fish from their housetops until they are drowned. Later, they are turned into mosquitoes. The Navajo Myth shows how Coyote stole two Water Monster babies and brought on the flood by stealing from the Water Monster Mother. Water, in all of the stories, is a complement to Fire, a mysterious power that must be understood in order to be used properly.

Haida Grouped with the Tlingit and Tsimshian tribes of the Northwest Coast, the Haida were fine woodcarvers and house-builders whose carved totem poles and potlatches (feasts) became legendary. The name Haida was commonly given to the inhabitants of the Queen Charlotte Islands of British Columbia.

Great Spirit The Great Spirit has many names, including Great Mystery, Wakanda (Siouan) and Manito (Algonquian). The concept of a Great Spirit that is not a monotheistic deity is difficult for some to grasp, but this is the meaning given by Native Americans. It cannot be reduced to theology and it encompasses many deities, forces, powers. Simply stated, it is the energy of life, the source of it, the heartbeat of all things. Thus, this emanation of power is, or can be felt in living and non-living forms. The Native American belief is that all matter is animate, all things live or have that potency and potential. The life-force that connects each to all and all to each is the Great Spirit.

Holy People Given the name Yei by the Navajo, the
Holy People form a pantheon of deities including Father
Sun, Mother Earth, and their sons, Monster Slayer and
Born of Water. The deities are creatures (Coyote), men
(First Man), and insects (Locust) as well as plants (Corn),
and phenomena (Rainbow).

Horned Serpent A universal Amerindian concept of
unification, the horned and feathered serpent is the deity
from which Snake is the earthly representative. Great Snake,
as he is called by many Southwestern Tribes, is associated
with thunder, lightning, and rain. Certain ceremonies of the
Navajo are not practiced until the cold time comes, Winter,
when Great Snake is asleep. Symbolically, Feathered Serpent
unifies Earth and Sky, by being an amalgam of scale and
feather. His power, therefore, is both earthly and heavenly.

Hozhoni The Navajo concept of oneness, of being at
peace with all things in the universe, is called *Hozhoni*. It
means harmony within and without, above and below,
all around, a circle of unbroken peacefulness of which man
is merely a part.

Hummingbird Sacred bird of the Navajo and other Southwestern tribes, Hummingbird is believed to be a medicine person, the first healer of birds. The sound of Hummingbird's wings reminds The People of little bells ringing in the wind.

Indian When Christopher Columbus miscalculated his location in the West, thinking he had arrived in the East, he named the first people he saw on the Bahamian Islands of the Caribbean "Indians" (India = Indian). The rest is what we call history, or error. The first people of Turtle Island called themselves, in their myths, The People, and that is what most tribal names, once dis-entangled from their European/English mistranslation, mean.

Indian Bread Many different flour or meal derived breads are used by Native Americans. Some of these are fragile and papery, such as Zuni *Piki* bread. Others, like Navajo fry bread, are flat, slightly-risen pan breads. Conventional loaves baked in southwestern outdoor adobe ovens are also commonly referred to as Indian bread. The Bannock Indians of the West cooked a root-bread which has been passed down through the generations and today is known simply as bannock.

Jamaica On the second voyage of Christopher Columbus (and on his fourth voyage), he stayed among the Arawaks on the island of Jamaica. The Arawaks named it *Xaymaca*, meaning "land of wood and water." Columbus called the island paradise, "the fairest island that eyes have beheld." However, in their search for gold and in establishing the island as a colony, the Spanish liquidated the very people who had besfriended them.

Kiowa The Kiowa language is related to Tanoan, one of the Pueblo languages. Kiowa myths suggest an ancient Southwest origin, but they have always lived or near the Plains. Hunters, primarily, the Kiowa range was from the Missouri River in Montana, as far south as Texas and down to Mexico.

Kiva The sacred ceremonial chamber of the Pueblo Indians, the Kiva is a place of meditation, prayer, ceremony and rite of passage. It is sometimes characterized as an "emergence place," representing one of the earlier stages of Native American mythological life. The Kiva contains aspects of all the primordial elements: earth, air, water and fire.

Kwakiutl The Kwakiutl are a tribe of the Pacific Northwest, whose identification with the life cycle of the salmon made it a permanent part of their mythology. Their ability to carve totem poles, the heraldic symbols of their culture, is well known. They are related linguistically and culturally to the Tsimshian and Salish on the mainland of British Columbia, which is the home of all three tribes. Their religion was centered around aquatic creatures that were their sustenance.

Magpie   One of the many Native American tricksters, Magpie is an audacious, clever, fun-loving, trick-playing bird. He has been known to hoodwink Coyote by appealing to Coyote's vanity. Some tribes consider the Magpie's white and blue-black feathers sacred and use them in ceremonials.

Medicine   This is one of the most misused words in the Native American English vocabulary. In native tongue, "medicine" translated literally usually meant "mystery." A medicine man was, therefore, a mystery man. Most tribes made a distinction between a root/herb doctor and a great man of wisdom, though the two functions were frequently combined in the same person.

Mermaid (Moomah)   The Native American sea deity was fused, in the minds of European sailors and missionary people, with tales from Celtic and Anglo-Saxon lore. It was also often confused with mariners' stories of women singing in the moon-lit bays of strange and distant seaports. In Jamaican patois and folklore, *moomah* means "mother," which is identical to the Arawak myth of the Water Goddess, who protects the rivers that empty into the sea. This myth — porpoises and manatees notwithstanding — is certainly a universal one, found in Spanish, English, and other folktales.

Messiah   Around the turn of the century, Native Americans were seduced into thinking they, like the children of Israel, might be delivered from their oppressors, the Euro-American settlers. The myth of a Messiah is common in Native American mythology. The Feathered Serpent, in one incarnation, was thought to be a man with white skin and light-colored eyes. In Navajo origin tales, two white people arrived upon the plane of the fourth world, but soon vanished into the sky. The portent of this myth, like the Hopi *Pahana* legend, is that one day these white brothers would return and confer knowledge of a different kind upon The People. Handsome Lake, the 19th Century Iroquois prophet, was a reformed alcoholic whose vision led him to preach the word of God. His was a strictly non-combative ministry, based upon peace, acceptance, and brotherhood.

Moon Often cast in myths as Sun's sister or a cousin of Mother Earth, Moon is usually a female symbol. In Iroquois myths, Moon is Old Woman Diviner, who is always weaving a headstrap. When she gets up to stir her pot of boiled corn, her cat unravels the headstrap, and she has to start all over again. The moon as a giver of light, a planetary body, is usually described as a thing made of white shell, or white stone, related to the planetary sun. Both bodies of light are differentiated in the myths from the character of the Sun or Moon, the myth-figure who has both godly and human attributes.

Nahuatl The Nahuatl were the Aztec of Aztlan, who came from the legendary North and settled in and around the Southwest, particularly in Texas, New Mexico and Arizona. Originally, the Nahuatl were known *Chichimeca*, the People of the Dog.

Navajoland This large reservation comprises more than fifteen million acres in what is called the Four Corners of the Southwest, where Colorado, Utah, New Mexico, and Arizona meet. It is a magical, yet often desolate landscape of mesas, plains, buttes, wind-sculpted cliffs, high mountains, and dry deserts.

Oklahoma The name *Oklahoma* was coined by a Choctaw leader as a translation of "Indian Territory." In Choctaw it means "Red Men."

Owl   The owl is a sacred, yet contradictory bird in Native American mythology. In Kwakiutl myth, when this creature calls, it means someone is going to die. As messenger of death, the owl is not evil, but it can be foreboding. In the Pueblos along the Rio Grande in New Mexico, the owl is definitely a bird of dark omen. In the legendary moccasin game of the Navajo, the old stories tell of how Owl tried to hide the pebble under his wing to ensure that it would always be night. He was, however, caught cheating, and that is why night and day are divided equally.

Pascagoula   The Pascagoula Tribe, once residing at the mouth of Pascagoula Bay, Mississippi, were thought to have been absorbed by the Biloxi Indians. However, there are two other versions of their disappearance. In the oral versions of the legend of mass-suicide, the Pascagoula drown themselves in the Bay to avoid expatriation by the European settlers. However, printed versions of the tale indicate the mass drowning took place as a result of the inducement of the tribal water deity or mermaid. A story is also told of Ibo slaves, fresh from Africa, who are said to have marched singing into Dunbar Creek, on St. Simons, a Georgia Sea Island, to escape slavery. This story also exists among Seminole-blacks whose ancestors were runaway slaves from Georgia and South Carolina. The common thread in these stories is escape from oppression and expatriation. In the Caribbean Islands where Blacks and Indians escaped their white overseers by "taking to the bush" and sharing herbal and other survival secrets, there were also, no doubt, similar myths and legends.

Pollen The sacred pollen of the cornplant is used by a variety of tribes in their ceremonials. As a daily tribute and sun-blessing, corn pollen is used by Navajos, Apaches and Pueblos. The sacred grains were observed by Columbus as well as Captain John Smith. Flour blessings figure in pre-Christian and Christian mythology, and it has been suggested by some scholars that the *manna* of biblical lore is a lichen or pollen derivative. The Apaches called it *Hoddentin* and gathered the sacred grains from the tule plant. Apache medicine men said that it was good for human and animal consumption, as bears sought it and ate it as readily as people. Trails of battle were blessed by pollen, as well as the trail made in the sand by the rattlesnake.

Potawatomi The Potawatomi spoke a Chippewan dialect and lived in Wisconsin and along Lake Huron. They fought for the French until 1773; they fought the Americans during the Revolution; and they fought the English in the War of 1812. They were removed by the Americans to Iowa, Kansas, and Canada. According to their own records, their land rights may have extended as far east as Ohio and Pennsylvania.

Pueblo The term *pueblo* was first used by the Spanish Conquistadores to designate the Indians they found living in villages of mud, sand and stone. These communal people developed one of the most cooperative societies on Turtle Island, one that has lasted for hundreds of years. Today, the Pueblos of New Mexico and Arizona are the longest permanently lived-in settlements in North America.

Rabbit Rabbit was a sacred animal to the Mimbres as well as other southwestern tribes. The Menomini myth tells of the time of beginnings, when Flint mixed with Earth and Blood and changed into Rabbit, who then changed into Man.

Raven The Tlingit legend describes Raven as a shapeshifter, who makes himself into a small piece of dirt, which goes into the drinking water of the daughter of a rich man who keeps medicine bags of stars. Raven, disguised as dirt, gets the girl pregnant, and after her child is born, he throws the medicine bags up the smoke hole, giving birth to stars, moon and sun.

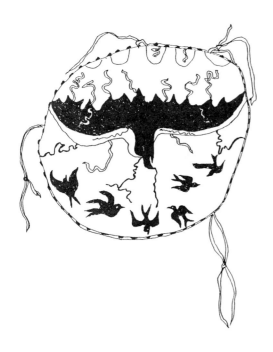

Sacred Color, Sacred Mountain, Sacred Flint, Sacred Ground In Native American cosmology, all things, animate and inanimate, possess life. The sacred colors may vary somewhat from tribe to tribe, but are usually an expression of the colors of the dawn, the rainbow or the setting sun (thus, blue, white, yellow, red, and black). Most tribes like the Cherokee, whose Bald Mountain figures in their mythology, have one or more sacred mountains, places on the Earth that reflect the origin or emergence stories. For the Navajo, Flint represents the armor of the Gods, the points of arrowheads; in short, Flint is very potent medicine. The Earth, as a Native American symbol, is the most sacred and the most primary. The matriarchal tribes — the Navajo, for instance, sometimes put greater faith in the Mother than the Father, and the myths show this.

Sauk and Fox An Algonquian tribe who lived in Illinois, Indiana, and, originally, Michigan. The Fox "branch" of the tribe once identified themselves to the French as part of the Fox Clan, and the name stuck.

Scarification For many of the Plains tribes in particular, as well as others in general, inflicting wounds on the body was an act of courage, faith, prayer, visionary power, and rank. The Sun Ceremony, among other acts of obeisance, involves hooking into the pectoral muscles and drawing upon them with great force. This is done in homage to the sun.

Seneca A part of the Iroquois Confederacy (Seneca, Cayuga, Onandaga, Oneida, Mohawk), these Mohegan people lived in northwestern New York.

Sequoyah This Cherokee man is credited with the invention of the Cherokee alphabet. Formally unschooled, he designed his alphabet without missionary assistance.

Seri The Seri are a Mexican Indian tribe, originally fishermen, whose language has roots in the Hokan family of the Southwest, California, and Middle America.

Shell Shells of all kinds are used in many ways by Native Americans. The archetypal money-belt of *wampum* was once common throughout Turtle Island. The cowrie shell was considered especially sacred by Plains and other tribes, not to mention African tribes, where until the mid-1950s, it was still being used as currency.

Sioux Originally, the Sioux were a group of closely related woodland tribes living west of the Chippewa in Wisconsin. In time, however, the Chippewa pushed them toward the Great Plains, where they adopted the nomadic hunting life.

Smoking Herb   (Tobacco)Next to corn, tobacco is the most sacred herb on Turtle Island. Used to treat disease, seal agreements, and for ceremonies of all kinds, tobacco originally came from the Guarani of South America, and found its way through the ancient trade routes of Turtle Island via Mexico and the Caribbean.

Spirit World   The concept of the spirit world in Native American religion and myth would seem to be almost identical to another dimension of time above or beyond this one, where the participants behave as they do here.

Star People In many Native American myths, stars figure as animals and people who have definite relations on Turtle Island. The Cherokee tale speaks of stars as turtles that give off sparks when the wind touches them. In Creek stories the stars are earth people who leave and go into the heavens.

Thirteen Fires This reference is linked to the original thirteen colonies. In Native American parlance "fires" meant villages, or council fires, one for each colony.

Totem The word *Totem* came originally from a Chippewa concept meaning "brother, sister kin." Often, an animal that was the main subsistence of the clan was revered as its benefactor, and became its totem. The clan patron spirit, then, was a guardian, animal or otherwise, that looked after the clan.

Trickster Creator and destroyer, affirmer and negator, the Trickster becomes a kind of animal metaphor for the plight of human beings. He is at once animal, human, hero, clown, devil and fool who shows us the folly and force of our divine and profane ideas of life.

Virgin Mother The Oglala Sioux called her White Buffalo Woman, but she has been given other names by other tribes. She is, for most Amerindians, the embodiment of Mother Earth, the watchful, nurturing, protective Mother of the Americas, who, mixed somehow with Christian imagery, is most universally known as the Virgin of Guadalupe. The Virgin Mary, brought to the new world by Europeans, was a symbol of beauty and compassion. Native Americans conceptualized her as the image of Mother Earth.

Wichita This tribe was part of the Caddoan Confederacy in the area that was originally Kansas, but which extended from Oklahoma into Texas.

Wind   There are good and bad winds in Native American myths. Geronimo called upon Winds of Power to surround and protect his warriors. Navajo myths speak of Messenger Wind who warns the Hero Twins when they are in danger. Wind People in many of the stories are propitiated and brought into harmony with the Earth people, who summon them in the hope of utilizing their power.

Wounded Knee   Most historians agree that the outcome of the massacre of Native Americans at Wounded Knee Creek near the turn of the century drew the final curtain on the drastic events that permanently confined Indians to reservation life. The Native American population that existed at the time of Columbus — some estimated 850,000 people — had, by Wounded Knee, dwindled to 250,000. In 1973, Wounded Knee became the site of action again, when militant members of the Oglala Sioux of Pine Ridge took over the town and demanded their rights be recognized. The militants held the town for 71 days, but though the siege was even more famous, world-wide, than the first Wounded Knee, the result was the same — promises lost in rhetoric.

ACKNOWLEDGMENTS

The following Native American, American and Jamaican storytellers gave me the bones, and in some cases the flesh, of the stories in this book:

James Clois Smith, Jr.: *The Bread Eaters.* The story was told to me by Jim in Biloxi, Mississsippi and later corroborated by the author (*A Treasury of Southern Folklore*, Edited by B.A. Botkin, Crown Publishers, 1949). There are other variations of the story, one of them published by me in the book *Runners*, Sunstone Press, 1983.

Sweet-Sweet: The Arawak. Told and recorded on tape in 1986, this narrative poem crosses racial and mythic lines, from Arawak to African. Sweet-Sweet, a Jamaican storyteller, claims to have seen the mermaid himself, though he believes the story was passed from one generation to another. I recorded it at Blue Harbour, Jamaica, West Indies.

Robert Boissiere and Michael Strange: *The Mother and the Child.* The story was told two different ways by two different people, neither of whom knew each other. Later, to simplify the theme, and after visiting the Sea of Cortez where the stories took place, I fused the two narratives into one.

Sid Hausman: *The Raven Watcher* (part one). The story was told to me by my brother at Highlands University in Las Vegas, New Mexico in 1967. It was "authenticated" by Dr. Irma E. Schuster of the history department.

Loren Straight Eagle Plume Toledo: *The Raven Watcher* (part two). This poem is published, as written, in Loren's words with the editor's addition of one line "And everyone agreed it was a good sign."

Paul Metcalf: *Beyond Bald Mountain*. The story is presented from Paul's classic work on the Cherokees, *Will West*, and was abridged with the permission of the author. The original mythological fragment came from the anthropologist, James Mooney. Paul Metcalf, the author of numerous books, happens to be the great-grandson of Herman Melville and wishes it known that he is not a Native American writer. He also wishes to make it clear that the title, *Beyond Bald Mountain* came from the editor.

Keewtagoushkum, Chief Logan, Little Turtle, Red Jacket, Cornplanter, Metea, Black Hawk: *Brother, Listen to Me*. These were originally given as speeches by Native American elders and chiefs. I found them in a text published in 1834 and abridged them for *The Sun Horse*. To my knowledge most of these have not appeared in book form since their original publication.

James Mooney: *The Messenger*. This text, published in different form in 1896 as *The Ghost Dance Religion and the Sioux Outbreak of 1890*, appears in this new narrative format for the first time.

Irene Toya: *Deer Boy*. Told to the author by Irene, the story was later corrected in typescript by her. It is an exact portrayal of an event at San Juan Pueblo which happened to Irene's son, J.J., and it is used here with her permission. The "pencil studies" for the illustrations were suggested by Irene.

Jay (Bluejay) de Groat: *The Sun Horse*. Told to the author by Jay, this story is the living myth of a Navajo poet and painter.

To all of these gracious people, my deepest appreciation for sharing their wisdom with me.

Selected Bibliography

Hausman, Gerald

    Meditations with Animals. Santa Fe: Bear & Co., 1986.

    Navajo Nights. Santa Fe: Sunset Productions, 1992.

    Meditations with the Navajo. Santa Fe: Bear & Co., 1988.

    Stargazer. Silver Lake: Lotus Light, 1988.

    Stargazer. Santa Fe: Sunset Productions, 1992.

    Turtle Dream. Santa Fe: Mariposa, 1989

    Native American Animal Stories. Santa Fe: Sunset Productions, 1992.

    Ghost Walk. Santa Fe: Mariposa, 1991.

    Ghost Walk. Santa Fe: Sunset Productions, 1992.

    Turtle Island Alphabet. New York: St. Martin's, 1992.

    The Gift of the Gila Monster: Navajo Ceremonial Tales. New York: Simon & Schuster, 1992.

Littlebird, Larry.

    A Pueblo Indian Child's Christmas. Santa Fe: Circle Film Productions, 1991.

    Hunter's Heart. Santa Fe: Sunset Productions, 1992.

Metcalf, Paul

    Genoa: A Telling of Wonders. Albuquerque: University of New Mexico Press, 1991.

    Patagoni. Penland: The Jargon Society, 1971.

    Apalache. Berkeley: Turtle Island Foundation, 1976.

    Will West. Lenox: The Bookstore Press, 1973.

Momaday, N. Scott
House Made of Dawn. New York: HarRow, 1985.
The Names. Tucson: University of Arizona Press, 1987.
The Way to Rainy Mountain. Albuquerque:
University of New Mexico Press, 1976.
The Ancient Child. New York: HarRow, 1989.
Storyteller. Santa Fe: Sunset Productions, 1992.

Ortiz, Simon J.
Earth Power Coming. Tsaile: Navajo Community
College Press, 1990.

Rosen, Kenneth
The Man to Send Rainclouds. New York: Vintage Books,
1975.

Waters, Frank
Book of the Hopi. New York: Penguin, 1977.
Masked Gods: Navajo and Pueblo Ceremonialism.
Athens: Swallow/Ohio University Press, 1950.
The Man Who Killed the Deer. Athens: Swallow/Ohio
University Press, 1942.
Hopi. Santa Fe: Sunset Productions, 1992.

Zelazny, Roger
Eye of Cat. Santa Fe: Sunset Productions, 1992.
Eye of Cat. New York: Avon Books, 1991.

Photo and Illustration Credits:

The author wishes to thank Charles Dailey and The Institute of American Indian Arts Museum for help in preparing this book. Images are used courtesy of the museum and the many individual artists who attended the Institute. Information regarding museum art can be obtained by writing:

The Institute of American Indian Arts
Post Office Box 20007
Santa Fe, New Mexico 87504

The author wishes to thank Mina Yamashita, the designer of *The Sun Horse*, as well as one of the main illustrators.

He also wishes to thank Sunstone Press for many of the notecard images displayed here. A free catalog can be obtained by writing:

Sunstone Press
Post Office Box 2321
Santa Fe, New Mexico 87504-2321

PAGE	TITLE/SOURCE
Cover	Plains Indian Horseman, Yeffe Kimball Collection, I.A.I.A
7	The Blanchard Turtle, print, Ross LewAllen
9	Tewa deer symbol, rendering from pottery design, Hausman Collection
15	Leopard Cowrie, photograph, Bobbe Besold
16-18	Whales, illustration, Marjorie Zakian
19	*Creation Story*, painting, Solomon McCombs, I.A.I.A.
21	Turtle Motif, pen and ink drawing, Mariah Fox
22	Arawak Petroglyph, pen and ink drawing, Mariah Fox
23	Mermaid, brush drawing, Mina Yamashita
24	Arawak Turtle, pen and ink drawing, Mariah Fox
25	Skin with Raven and Bear, Paw photograph, I.A.I.A.
27	A Raven Totem at Yan, photograph, Edward S. Curtis
28	Fish Motif, brush drawing, Mina Yamashita
29	A Koskimo House, photograph, Edward S. Curtis
30	*Virgin of Guadalupe*, drawing, Andrea Bacigalupa, Sunstone Notecard Collection
32,35	Bird, Sunset, brush drawings, Mina Yamashita
40	Water Beetle, pen and ink drawing, Mina Yamashita
42	Arrow, pen and ink drawing, Mariah Fox
43	Eagle, brush drawing, Mina Yamashita
44	Bear Tracks, pen and ink drawing, Mariah Fox
45	*Man In The Earth*, Southwest basket motif, W.E. Channing & Co.
48	Plains Pipes, photograph, Yeffe Kimball Collection, I.A.I.A
50	*The Black Horse*, painting, Antoine Tzapoff, Sunstone Notecard Collection
51	Photo #UN 21.01, Museum of Indian Arts and Culture/Laboratory of Anthropology, Santa Fe, NM
52	*Playing Fox*, Peabody Museum, Harvard University

BOOKS AND TAPES FROM LOTUS LIGHT

To Order, send full payment for each title ordered,
along with shipping/handling charge of 10% of TOTAL ORDER.

(Minimum Shipping charge $3.00)

Wisconsin Residents add 5 1/2% sales tax.

Send to:

LOTUS LIGHT PUBLICATIONS

Post Office Box 325-SH

Twin Lakes, Wisconsin 53181

Dealer and Wholesale Inquiries are Welcomed.

Request our complete catalog of Native American books,
tapes, and smudge sticks and supplies.

The Sacred Tree

was created by the Four Winds Development Project, a native American inter-tribal group, as a handbook of Native Spirituality for the indigenous peoples all over the Americas and the world. Through the guidance of the elders, native values and traditions are being taught as the primary key to unlocking the forces that will move native peoples on the path of their own development. The elders have prophesied that by returning to traditional values, native societies can be transformed. This transform- ation would then have a healing effect on the entire planet.

Paper, 7 3/4 x 8 1/2, 88 pp
ISBN 0-941524-58-2   **$9.95** RETAIL

OTHER WORK BY GERALD HAUSMAN

STARGAZER: A Native American Inquiry
     Into Extraterrestrial Phenomena

A Navajo stargazer (medicine man), a French ufologist and an American poet join forces to probe one of the strangest mysteries in the Southwest. The true story of one man's emergence through Native American ritual into the world of psychic and extraterrestrial experience. From the peaceful pueblos on the Rio Grande to jungle ruins in Cozumel, the tale focuses on myth and personal experience.

BOOK: Paper, $5_{1/2}$ x $8_{1/2}$, 219 pp
ISBN 0-914955-03-9   **$9.95** RETAIL

TAPE: Narrated and read by the author/Music
ISBN 0-92402-00-6   **$10.95** RETAIL

NAVAJO NIGHTS   Gerald Hausman
Read by Gerald Hausman with music.
A wonderful compilation of Navajo healing stories, told with passion and understanding of the Navajo tradition.
approx. 50 minutes
ISBN 1-56431-020-5   **$10.95** RETAIL

NATIVE AMERICAN ANIMAL STORIES
Gerald Hausman
Read by Gerald Hausman with music.
Stories collected and wonderfully narrated from the Navajo, Cheyenne, Hopi, Kwaikiutl, Tlingit, and Iroquois tribes.
aprox. 53 minutes
ISBN 1-56431-021-3   **$10.95** RETAIL

GHOSTWALK Gerald Hausman
Native American Tales of the Spirit
Read by Gerald Hausman with music.
Captivating tales of shadows and *The lost time / When one thing becomes another.*
approx. 40 minutes
ISBN 0-929402-11-1   **$10.95** RETAIL

TURTLE ISLAND ALPHABET
Gerald Hausman
Read by Jill Momaday with music.
A rich and poetic anthology of Native American myths and stories.
approx. 180 minutes
ISBN 1-56431-035-0   **$10.95** RETAIL